EXCESS BAGGAGE

Sarah-Jane Dunwoody

Published by Sarah-Jane Dunwoody
Email: rosetimaru@gmail.com

First published 2025
© 2025 Sarah-Jane Dunwoody

ISBN 978-0-473-73212-7

A catalogue record for this book is available from the
National Library of New Zealand.

For Bryn

"It is not in the stars to hold our destiny

but in ourselves. "

– William Shakespeare

Preface

Written in the Stars ☆

Perched high up in the leafy tree branches, a tui opened up
its voice boxes and warbled out an eerie omen song, as if
calling in the codes for the day. Taking the seat offered at a
wooden kitchen table, I settled myself into the room. The
garden outside filtered the sunlight streaming in through
wide windows, throwing foliage patterns onto surfaces in the
room. The owner of the kitchen loaded a cassette into the
portable tape player and pressed down on two buttons to
start recording this meeting. She introduced the date, gave
her name and began to tell me my future. This was the
psychic reading from a medium named Mary who professed
to see it all written in the stars.

There were four of us in the mid 1980s who had been
close friends throughout our late teenage years. Our

schooling was finishing and we were being let loose into the adult world. With varying degrees of belief, but with eager regularity, we would find the next 'best' recommended psychic in town and spend our hard earned pay packets having our fortunes told. The readings were predictive and foretold the possible opportunities that were going to crop up for us in the coming months and years. Whether we believed in the predicted outcome or not, having one solid hour focusing on oneself definitely created a positive exercise to assist with decision making. It was teaching us to look at our emotions and reactions to some of the big looming questions we were asking ourselves about the direction our lives were taking.

Throughout the reading, loved ones from beyond the veils, unknown ancestors from the other side, and supposed guides would drop in with titbits of advice. This always gave me a sense of comfort and wonder that there was the possibility of company from other realms, beings who appeared to have our best interests at heart.

The readings done for me often told of distant places across water. Living in New Zealand our culture is well known for taking on the big OE (overseas experience) in our late teens to early twenties. Really, there was a high chance this sort of information was a given for a Kiwi youngster and I often thought it seemed a relatively easy prediction to give.

Travel was something I yearned to do though. I believed there were destinations I needed to visit and famous sites I wanted to stand amongst. My Mum had travelled far and wide through her life and she had instilled in me always the greatness of seeing the world. Also, having read so much throughout my childhood, I wanted to go and experience first hand the scenes I had read about, curious to see if the descriptions matched up to my imagination.

Everybody must surely, at some time in their life, question what we are put on planet earth for. The enchantment of being able to shortcut some life lessons and have somebody give us answers through a predictive reading was quite tempting. We were adults to look at, but we were only teetering on the edge of ending childhood - struggling to try to forge ahead with our adult selves and to make some of those more mature decisions. Not trusting that real grownups around us were ever going to give us the right advice, we were happier with direction from what we believed might be coming from the other side. Possibly we were just earning someone a nice piece of pocket money, but I felt no harm was ever done.

To hand the decisions over to another and to have the answers come forward from the ethers piqued our curiosity. It made us wonder what else was out there in the never-never to be discovered. This was an era before the internet and for querying young minds, mediumship gave a sense that there was more to life than we had been taught to believe. In many people's mindsets it was also frowned upon as an occupation and so of course youth will always be attracted to this kind of energy.

Fortune-telling equally fascinated and frightened us as we perceived its power to control the outcome of our decisions. In truth, predictions for fortune, romances and holidays abroad were what we were really keen to hear about. We were working hard to bring those things into our lives and we wanted confirmation that it was okay to do so. Having lived in a tiny country community and with a whole world out there to discover, we were storing up some bravery to begin exploring, by hearing of some positive outcomes that could be ours to claim.

On this particular day at the kitchen table there were two pieces of information that came channelled through as part of the reading and they resonated crystal clear to me. I have remembered them to this day. Maybe this is just because I recognised them as part of the life contract I had signed up for and therefore they were already known to me at a deeper secret level.

The first gem brought through from Mary, sitting upright in her chair and staring into space, was when she stated, "I see you are going to meet a teacher". Within my circle of friends I had always held the hippy archetype. A girl who grew up on a beach, enjoyed the outdoors, was vegetarian, grew my hair long, didn't really follow fashion. I was intrigued to know that a teacher of some importance was going to appear in my life. My mind quickly darted to different scenarios. Was it to be a quiet meditative saffron robed monk, or a bearded gnarled lungi clad figure, or since I enjoyed dance and movement, possibly even a yoga teacher? With travel foretold in my future, I made a note to myself to be ready and open to meeting this great teacher.

In the 1980s many people around me were starting to break away from Christianity and explore the possibility of seeking out their own guru/master/teacher to follow. These figures would be expected to bring through teachings to assist us to alight upon our true life paths. With some of the spiritual innocence of those times, we had not yet fathomed that we can each begin to find that knowledge within ourselves, with a little inner work.

Mary carried on with the reading and the second piece of information that came through and resonated loudly were the words, "You are going to do some writing at some stage in your life and be given the time, space and support to do so".

Written in the Stars

The urge to write has always only held a subtle influence in my life. Anyone who loves reading, must surely hanker a little to add at least one more book to the world. How fabulous is it that we can never run out of books to read in one lifetime. In fact, it makes me now wonder how many ghosts or energies sit in our public libraries finishing off all the reading they couldn't get done in their human physical lifetime.

However, I never did write much, although the thought would occasionally cross my mind. Then in 2019, I found myself avoiding some housework and wanting to sit out in the sun, so I sat down with a laptop and began to write this story. Three hours evaporated as I climbed into my brain and dug around for some words and pushed them into sentences and completed some paragraphs. It was an early spring day with gentle warmth in the sun and I typed away on my little computer enjoying the experience of taking a trip back in time, connecting with the younger me. Speed typing is one of my superpowers and I can tap out my thoughts as quickly as they arise.

Written in the Stars

I felt quite excited that I had sat myself down long enough to try some writing. I immediately thought back to the psychic reading I had gone to over 30 years before and suddenly wondered if the time had come for the writing to begin just as had been predicted all those years ago. Gracefully entering my fifties, I felt I wanted to get this story finally down onto paper - or at least onto a computer screen. Suddenly, like a sign from the ancestors who had written in times of quill and ink, the computer screen literally turned into a giant ink blot. Before me was a black and white blotchy mess. That was it - the little cheap computer had died a timely death and the screen had given up the ghost.

I sighed, packed up and investigated if it was worth trying to fix the computer or buy a new one - it was easier to put the writing career on hold. Life seemed to get busy and other priorities took over and I tucked away the thought of writing. Ego has a magnificent way of telling you how useless you would be at new ventures. Although it has a right to do so at times, to protect you from some foolish choices, I allowed it to influence me and agreed that I wasn't up for the challenge of being a writer.

Roll forward to October 2021 and what a different world we now live in. My comfortable job as a part time librarian changed overnight as we headed into our second tightly controlled countrywide lockdown due to humans' new nemesis the pandemic of Covid19. Yes, I had made it into the arena of books, albeit not as a writer. As a Library Assistant the customer service role dealing with the public was an eye opener, but the carer of the books role was a pretty happy place to be working.

The Covid-19 Delta Variant had hit New Zealand much later than many other countries and we were belatedly forced into mandated masks like much of the rest of the world. I live on the South Island and we came out of the hard lockdown earlier than the North Island. New working protocols were quickly cobbled together and suddenly my role at the library changed. I was now to be stationed in the foyer acting as mask police. Customers were required by law to wear masks and be signed into the premises. This was a new practice for the general public and somehow overnight it had become my job to educate them.

From the outset, I knew I was going to feel uncomfortable wearing a mask - who doesn't? The mental anguish of wearing one was experienced by most people, but I didn't expect the big physical reaction I had after wearing one longer than half an hour. A four hour shift at the library became unbearable to me as my eyes began to hurt, fatigue settled over me, my brain seemed to stall and become foggy, a headache began and then my chest would tighten occasionally as if I were at altitude. My lungs seemed to question if there was enough oxygen for the next full breath.

Whilst I stood in the library foyer and made sure patrons had signed into the building for contact tracing and had put their masks on, I felt a sense of disbelief that this was unfolding before me. I looked into the main library and watched my masked colleagues in the distance buzzing around their duties looking like muppets. Cover up the features of the bottom half of our human faces and we look just like puppets.

I wanted to scream with frustration and then giggle with mad laughter and anguish. Dumbed down, muffled and numbed was what the mask wearing felt like to me. As if kidnapped and gagged by a world gone much too crazy for my liking, I was absolutely struggling with this adaptation we were being asked to perform. It saddened and triggered me and made me feel ill.

I'm not an anti-masker. The science for now proves the benefits to all of us in a virus infected world. Governments and Health Departments were scrambling to see what they could do to keep communities safe. We have to try these things. But rather than struggle through for the foreseeable future, I decided to see it as the force that catapulted me to my next calling. After working masked shifts at the Library for three weeks I returned home one evening in a black mood and googled "writing a book". One of the first points I discovered is that "writing is a lonely, isolated pastime". Perfect. This is what I require from life right now. I read no further. Decision made, I handed in my resignation and gave the required two weeks' notice.

My boss and co-workers were a little shocked, but also showed understanding. It possibly looked as though I was just running away from the situation and in reality, I felt I wanted to. Running seems to work for me. The dutiful ritual of a "leaver's" morning tea was performed and the inevitable question was asked of me, "What are you going to do next?" I found myself replying, "I'm going to the garden shed to write". This, as it turns out, is the correct response from someone who is leaving a librarian role - my colleagues thought it was a noble choice. Once again those words from the past came back to haunt me. "You will write one day, and be given the time, space and support to do so"!

As I write this it's turbulent and rocky out there in every country right now. We are being forced to be locked up in our homes to be safe and then we are sent out again with mad new normals and told to get on with it, but be safe and kind. It's hard right now. I consider myself to be a spiritual person. I read and watch people online who are trying to teach a higher outlook to what is going on in these times. The big question seems to be, is this the ascension path for humanity? The enlightened ones thought they had this moment sighted. They felt prepared with the knowledge that they had seen something coming in for our world, to allow us to take our next step up. Unfortunately no-one seemed to have picked up and seen the true format it was all going to take. Hence to be centred, positive, joyful and peaceful through this pandemic is a big test for all humanity.

We are all looking to each other to find out what can help us through this. We are trying different tactics. Some are adhering to new rules. Some are doubting and questioning and railing against the strictures. Some of us are running away. Whatever path soothes the soul, is an okay and good choice for now. We need to find a way to just feel safe in each moment and hopefully slowly all the little moments will add up and this will pass.

I have recently felt refreshed by reading Ruth Jones's novels. She is a wonderful Welsh actress, script writer and novelist. Her novels are settings of my time. The stories are light, but to read of a pre-pandemic time gave me solace. It has given me an understanding of the habit that the seniors of our communities have, of dwelling in their pasts. I had previously wondered why they did this, but now with enough years under my belt and big fast changes happening in our world, I can see that taking a trip back through time somehow offers some respite from the daily grind.

So wherever you find yourself reading this I want to offer you and myself some comfort, by taking you on a little journey back through the decade of the 1990s and let's celebrate and enjoy a little yarn from the past. Two of my life mottos have been: firstly to not dwell on things in the past and secondly to have no regrets. I've mostly managed to adhere to my self-given rules, so it's funny that I now want to break the first one.

As destined in the stars, I was to meet a teacher, and now I seem to find myself with the time, space and support to write about how this came about.

1

A Street Full of Stars ☆

I watch a 1pm televised briefing. 71 new Covid-19 Delta cases to report. The Health and Education sector have now fallen under the "mandated vaccinations" groups. They must adhere to this to be able to hold down their jobs. Our cedarwood shed at the bottom of the garden is where I now come to write. The Kowhai tree that the shed sits under is in blossom and soon to become a mass of hot yellow flowers. Nature always offers hope.

In London, October 1990, a Drury Lane address held a famous quality to it. This narrow lane sitting at the heart of theatreland in the City of Westminster was where I liked to imagine that the majority of people who were making their way to their place of work each day were ballerinas, singers, dancers, actors and people of the arts world. Long limbed ballerinas with lovely extensions of their arms would stand on tiptoe and stretch out to open their doors. Actors from the Andrew Lloyd musical CATs would cross the lane with one large leap to easily arrive at their stage door. I was also on the lookout for a short, rotund character fitting my imagination of the 'Muffin Man' from the old classic nursery rhyme 'who lives on Drury Lane'.

Arriving at 186 Drury Lane ten minutes early for my interview, I was buzzed in through the bright blue door sporting a shiny brass door knob and letter box plate. The terraced building rising four stories high was clad in pale brick and seemed a magical English address to me. As it turns out, the elegant door knob and nameplate were to become part of my working duties, keeping the metal polished to a gleam, to maintain a great first impression for clients and visitors arriving at the door, waiting to be called up to enter the busy office.

Franklin Associates was a Public Relations company starting into its third year of trading and they were on the lookout for a word-processing star. I climbed the steep narrow staircase, ducked under the low ceiling entranceway, stepped onto the first floor landing and somehow managed to convince the Managing Director, Terrance Franklin, that I could fill said role. The fact that he roared with laughter when I mentioned I had just spent the previous four years as an administrator in the Royal New Zealand Air Force seemed to give me enough of an entertainment factor for him to be eager to employ me. He claimed he didn't know New Zealand was big enough to have an Air Force.

I was offered the job on the spot and started the next day. My large, shared working space was on the floor above Terry's immense office and one I shared with the writers. Smoke drifting around the room from cigarettes held at the corner of their mouths welcomed me as I came up the stairs. These men were working to deadlines and nicotine seemed to be what helped get them to the finish line. I cranked open the heavy sliding sash windows to be able to breathe a little easier and powered up the word processor.

They threw me hand written pieces and I would type them into the word processor at great knots. After a few edits were agreed we would be ready to go to print. The aim was to get the typed article for our client out into the evening post delivered to every major newspaper who would possibly take up the story and include it in their next issue. The printed article had to be folded into an envelope and postage stamped. After long hours typing, I always enjoyed these last mindless tasks to finish the day. Often even sitting on the floor in the middle of the office quickly folding A4 paper to fit the envelopes perfectly and tearing long strips of perforated stamps to run through water to activate the glue to stick to the corner. I would let my mind drift off to thoughts of what sightseeing I was up to next within London or further afield.

Clients were welcomed and heralded into Terry's expansive office by his Personal Assistant, Kate. He took pride of place as the boss, sitting behind the leather topped desk positioned in front of the two large windows overlooking the lane below. Grand olde world pictures adorned the walls and ashtrays were dotted around the room on side tables. Kate would bustle around settling the visitors into chairs and drinks were promptly provided. Tea or coffee was first poured and the meeting got underway. Then very quickly Kate would be called back into the office and asked to bring the corkscrew.

Many times in my employment at Franklin Associates I was called downstairs from my desk to enter Terry's office as he entertained the clients. "Here she is," he would sing out, grinning widely, clasping a large glass of wine. "Can you believe New Zealand is big enough to have an Air Force?" he would ask the bemused visitor. I was aged 23 and Terry was probably my favourite boss so far, making me happy to play along with the joke. My Dad had always concurred that my time in the Royal New Zealand Air Force would serve me well in my future and would look just fine on my Curriculum Vitae. I don't think this is exactly how he saw it playing out, but in some ways he was proved right.

It was easy being a Kiwi in London in the early 1990s. They seemed to like us, thought we were quaint and they didn't quite know where we fitted into the slowly disappearing class system of British culture. I had no idea where I fitted in to it either, so I just talked to anyone, watched carefully the Englishness unfold around me and tried to fit myself in without too many faux pas.

Surprisingly, from my recent New Zealand Air Force training, I had arrived in London with the right up-to-date administrative skills for the times. Word processors were fairly new in the business scene and it was a whole different world from the manual and electric typewriting that I had begun in my initial school and polytech training. It was, now looking back, the peak of my career having such advanced skills in the administrative world at that time. Within my office experience electric typewriters had been a huge step up from the manual typewriter, but to move into the digital world was pure magic for the typist. No more corrector tape and twink whiteout for typing errors, or fighting with smeary carbon paper to make the extra copies if required, all of which slows down the editing, to finished document stage. To be able to rehash existing writing and save documents to reuse them were amazing processes to get our heads around. I suffered horribly at first with eyesight strain, as apart from a television, which my family had never indulged in very much through my childhood, these were the first electronic screens we looked at for any length of time in a working day.

I worked hard, could type extremely fast and accurately even whilst holding a conversation on the telephone, my fingers pounding away at the keyboard and the phone's plastic chunky handpiece nestling on my shoulder. My colleagues in the office were impressed by this show of multi-tasking. These were old-school PR men who slumped over their desk with pen and paper and a cigarette burning in the ashtray to get their media marvels down and ready for me to type up. In the 1990s the typist was still sought after and we were now even becoming skilled at those newfangled electronic machines. We created the end result from penned jottings made by those creative minds and we turned that piece of writing into a professional looking legible printed document. A businessman would quail at the thought of ever learning how to type and completing a finished article himself.

In my high school days, back home in North Island New Zealand, my intimidating shorthand typing teacher had taught me how to touch type on a manual typewriter - hands under a bib so as to not see the keys I was striking. Too terrified to peek in fear of the wrath of the teacher, it skilled me to quickly memorise the finger positions for each key and become a fast touch typist. We had to bash away at the keys with equal strength of each finger, so as to make the ink mark of each letter the same uniform blackness throughout the document. A ding of a bell was the signal to grab the metal handle of the carriage return, slide it along and clunk the carriage firmly back to the start of the next line on the paper. Touch typing is a skill I have continued to enjoy to this very day. Was this in fact to be the very start of my skills needed for a writing career? If you are reading this book, then I imagine the answer has to be, yes it was.

This skill set had prepared me well for the frenzy of the PR office. Media stories were always worked to a short time frame. The pressure was on to get articles for the clients' latest story to all newspapers who may like to pick up and run the story. The writers lit cigarettes at a faster rate whilst they scribbled away. The boss sucked on his pipe and reminded us of timelines. Meanwhile Kate, his PA, was running to and fro with coffee or wine and jumping to all his requests. As all this unfolded, the word-processor star proceeded to gather everything into the finished format, printed out, folded into envelopes and postage stamped, ready to hit the evening post. Email did not exist yet and fax machines were still not being used to their fullest extent. I was the machine of this office.

Kate was a kind person to work with. She initially embraced having another female on the staff to deal with the foibles of these great businessmen. In the early 1990s our working lives were still very separated into roles for men and roles for women. I had left the RNZAF at a time when they were only just considering changing the rules to allow women to become pilots. PR was then still heavily a man's world and administration a female's world. Quite quickly Kate discovered the novelty of being able to pass on to me what she found to be the mundane duties in her day. This suited her new kudos as the 'senior administrator' and she seemed to enjoy having me as an underling. There was an administrative pecking order that needed to be adhered to. She pecked kindly and I was up for any task - I had a well paid job in London!

Pub lunches, drinks, meetings with glasses of wine - the London business world was a drinker's world and Kate was often found louder and rosier cheeked in the afternoons. She topped up the glasses for the boss and client and always accepted the offer to have one herself. Alongside keeping the door brass polished, I would also have to keep the wine rack stocked. I was given the petty cash from the locked blue tin and sent to the local supermarket. Franklin Associates were enthralled when I started coming back with bottles of New Zealand wine. It came within budget, it was good on the palate and it tickled their fancy that New Zealand was also big enough to have a wine industry. Here was another entertaining quip to be used on the clients by Terry.

To start with, in my innocence, I would take up the offer of the lunch time drink, but soon realised that I then suffered for the afternoon, trying to overcome the sleepiness and fuzzy head while still getting the required work output done. I partook less and less in the alcohol during the workday venture. Thank goodness my loveable drink-loaded boss Terry caught a bus to and from work each day. The entertainment happened every evening with Kate trying to pry Terry away from his desk and get his tall frame down the stairs with his briefcase in hand, in time for him to go and sober up on the bus during his one hour trip home.

Lunchtimes were a delight with the close proximity of Covent Garden. Interesting buskers, strolling tourists, local workers lunching, an eclectic covered market and beautiful shops surrounding a large cobbled square, highlighted with buildings of gorgeous old architecture. I would grab a superb sandwich from the small Italian cafe at the bottom of our building and wander off into the streets to be entertained by people. So many people. I had grown up in the Bay of Plenty, NZ on a long stretch of white sandy beach with crashing Pacific surf and not very many humans. On other days I would head in the opposite direction and take in a cafe and a quick look around the British Museum.

A Street Full of Stars

Weekends were free for me to pull out my battered copy of the London A-Z and hone my map reading skills as I worked out the underground (or tube) system and walked vast areas of London. I did have to regularly seek out parks to keep my connection with nature, without which I just cannot thrive. Squirrels enthralled me, as in New Zealand they had only featured in picture books and children's stories and I loved that they lived up to their descriptions.

Whilst working in Drury Lane, I lived in several different flats with English people and I found them great company. They were my training ground for what it was to live an English life - frequenting a local pub, eating large Sunday lunches, trying to dry washing when there was not much sun or daylight hours available each day, trying to keep warm in freezing conditions and pretending to like the bands they were all into and I had never heard of.

One loveable flat street address, reminding me of my favourite childhood biscuits, was Shrewsbury Mews in Notting Hill Gate. This was a tiny three story apartment which I shared with two kind English guys who were quiet and taught me to play chess. The next flat was in a truly awful building, but in a marvellous location just off the grandiose Marble Arch. My bedroom was damp and freezing and looked out onto a windowless brick wall of the building next door; it was barely heated by a dangerous old two bar electric heater. In the kitchen we used to turn the oven on in the evenings and at weekends and crowd around its open door to try and warm ourselves up.

I wandered frequently through Hyde Park just across the way and caught the red double decker buses down Oxford Street to my work. In the evening I would often jump off the bus early on the way home and walk the street to admire the amazing shop window frontages and take a shortcut through Selfridges Department Store and out their backdoor to my street. It all felt quintessentially English to me. Moving countries creates within you a childlike call to learning again. You are absorbing new signs and smells and nuances all day long and it is very invigorating. As a traveller it means you can do the cheapest of things and be entertained by just watching all this new culture pass you by.

And so for these first eight months I slowly found my place in London within both social and working life. It was a long winter and more often than not soft rain fell past the window as I worked. But there was always the friendly, clever humour of the English banter happening around me. I settled into the admin role easily and was the energetic youngster of the team.

2

Co-Star ☆

New Zealand has watched with some degree of horror the unfolding of mandated vaccines coming into law around the world. In my eyes, our small country could not follow such a harsh reality and yet as the turmoil and fear of the pandemic swirls on, our beautiful land of the long white cloud now too has opted to follow these reforms. I pass my herb garden on the way down to the cedarwood shed and I admire their strength to vigorously grow with the least amount of gardener assistance. Let us learn from the plants.

I don't remember our first meeting, and yet this is the person who was to instigate many large changes in my life and prove himself to be an important co-star to my part in the play here on Earth.

Claude was a political freelance writer who was contracted to Franklin Associates whenever his style of story was needed for a particular client. He always sat himself in the far corner of the room and got on quietly with his work - being rather aware I assume, that he was paid for every minute he was on site.

His trim figure was always neatly dressed, complete with a large umbrella in preparation for an average London day sprinkled with rain. One of the cutest shops close to where I worked was on a corner of New Oxford Street near Drury Lane, selling only umbrellas and walking sticks. Looking as if it had stepped out of a Dickens novel, the shop took up the whole corner plot, with the umbrellas displayed in the mahogany wood framed windows flanking both streets. Lovely old fashioned sign writing above and below the windows was highlighted with brass and looked as though it was original to the 1800s. I imagined it would have been the sort of shop where Claude bought his umbrellas.

Being quietly spoken, until something caught his fancy, Claude would then chortle with laughter quite loudly and it always surprised me. I discovered later that he had gone off to boarding school from age eight and that the

36

experience had done a lot to shape who he was. This explained the times when there appeared in him a boyish glee of laughing his head off in unsuitable moments when amused. Other times he was very solemn and had possibly, also at boarding school, learnt not to show too much emotion for fear of jibes. He fitted my ideal of the classy English gentleman and I started to enjoy his company more and more.

To start with I just thought of him as another of the writers in the office and the nine year gap in our ages left him slightly out of my field of interest. I had recently been through a relationship breakup and so wasn't looking for love. I felt a little shy around him and that signalled to me that he could possibly be more interesting than my other co-workers and I wondered if I could impress him enough, that he may become a friend. There would be many weeks when he wasn't around the office and suddenly he would be back inhouse working on some projects and it would then strike me that these were the more fun days at work.

Claude gently teased Kate and she adored him. They regularly lunched together and eventually I would get the odd invite to join them. We would choose a restaurant in the area and having Kate with us just meant it was a nice friendly, chatty lunch. I was always a little overwhelmed by his company, as I didn't feel very worldly and worried about trying to fit into the London way of life. Kate would prattle on about everything under the sun and Claude would throw in some intelligent anecdotes and I would agonise over what was the correct thing to order for lunch.

He was well travelled, and I had a few different countries under my belt. Throughout the work day we would take the odd break and share stories of where we had been and the countries we still wanted to go exploring. The day we spoke about Tibet I felt a bolt of lightning cross the room between us.

There were only the two of us in the office and Claude had swung his chair around to face me. When he mentioned Tibet was on his list, it threw me back to the first time I had seen a postcard picture of the Potala Palace when

I was only small. Looking at the picture, there had flashed about me a moment of recognition and knowing about this building, and I understood without a doubt that I would see it again in my lifetime.

Yet over the years coming out of childhood, I had forgotten all about this destination - I had not been planning any near future visit. There were too many closer countries on my new doorstep to go off and discover. Tibet was so far away and rather a hassle to get to as a tourist. You had to visit with an organised guided tour as it was a complicated country to gain access to since the Chinese takeover.

Claude, with his quiet determination, said he had plans to visit Tibet as a gift to himself when he turned 40. 1998 was going to be the year that he visited the area he had studied at university. An Englishman with an open mind to Buddhism was an intriguing mix for a girl from Papamoa Beach who had been told she was going to meet a teacher and had experienced a childish 'knowing' that the Dalai Lama's Potala Palace was somehow a feature in her life!

Co-Star

We were interrupted by colleagues returning back upstairs to their desks after a boozy lunch and I had to drag myself away from the image in my mind of the high walls and many small windows of that mysterious palace in its mountainous setting and return to the daily task of typing.

Claude turning back to his desk said in his very proper London accent, "Oh and maybe when I go, I'll take you with me". We laughed and settled back to work. That's seven years off I thought to myself - there is no way that will happen.

3

Solasta - (Scottish, meaning

Luminous or Shining) ☆

No jab, no job is being shouted at us through the media.
Vaccinate, vaccinate, vaccinate is an ongoing cry we hear
and it is being demanded of us everywhere we turn. Less
kindness in the messages out there now. I have played the
game and consented to the vaccination. Our intelligent
bodies deal with a lot of rubbish that we nonchalantly ingest
and inhale through our lifetime. I ask my intelligent body to
do the best it can with this next poison and ignore it if need
be.

With my first long English winter drawing to a close,
I was starting to experience the SAD (seasonal affective
disorder) state a body can reach when not experiencing
enough sunlight hours. The afternoons darkened quickly

with night falling from around 4pm, and the lack of light and constant cold that cut through my body were taking their toll on me. Running alongside my environment gloom was some emotional turmoil that I had tucked away, hoping I could just power through without letting it affect me.

My relationship with an Air Force chef who had followed me to the UK had ended in London. I had initially left New Zealand with a girlfriend to do one of the sought after bus tours around Europe. She was wanting a last ditch hurrah before getting serious with her man. I claimed I wanted a holiday, but in hindsight I was on the run from my relationship. This became pretty obvious when, on returning to the UK from our carefree three months touring, while my friend went home, got engaged and married in due course, I cashed in my ticket home and decided to stay put and get work in London. "Come join me," I wrote in letters to my boyfriend back home in New Zealand.

He gave up his chef career with the forces, flew out to join me and promptly fell in love with someone he worked with at his new job. Probably the biggest shock was that he had found the impetus to leave me before I had the courage to end our partnership. We had previously taken the move into a de facto relationship and lived in married quarters on the Air Force base for two years. For those initial years of our relationship we were really happy. We had met on an Air Force exercise in Vanuatu, spent a month travelling through Mexico, had a few adventures on his motorbike and owned two kittens and a dog together, but we were in our early 20s and still being created as adults and we had started to stifle each other. The energy of "us" had petered out.

After the breakup there was the new job at Franklin Associates, new flats and friends, a new city lifestyle and a quick visit from my parents. I ploughed on living and loving all of this. But an emotional fallout was happening in the background and I needed to do some adjusting and take some time for introspection as there was a sense of failure within myself. I decided to use a tried and tested solution that seems to work for me - I ran.

A small advert in the free weekly TNT magazine that I had picked up at Marble Arch Tube Station one grey skied

Monday morning on my way to the office, advertised a vacancy in the Highlands of Scotland. There were positions available working for a small watersports centre, complete with accommodation, a bar and a cafe/restaurant. The outdoors called to my soul and I felt a desperate need to get me out of the city and go and stretch and explore somewhere closer to nature. I rang the telephone number that evening and was offered the job for the summer season.

After working eight months at Franklin Associates I felt awfully awkward telling Terry that I needed to go off and do some more of my travels. He gruffly told me he had always expected it and off I was to go, hit the road and experience some more of the world. But, he added, he would have me back anytime I returned to London. Wow that was a result I hadn't seen coming.

Because 'backpacker' was the label I had given myself living on the other side of the world, I had resisted the urge to buy very much over my time in London. Packing to move was easy and I gave away a few books and clothes to flatmates so that once again everything I owned fitted in the one bag. I booked my long train journey up to the Scottish highlands and went to the electronics centre of London, Tottenham Court Road, to buy a walkman to listen to music for company. This only needed to be strapped on my body and didn't need to fit in my bag. I treated myself to the latest Sony sport version in a very modern outrageous bright yellow colour and with this new purchase my few cherished tapes were played ad infinitum.

I hopped off the train in the small village of Kingussie in Spey Valley and was met by Sally, who drove me to their Boathouse Restaurant on the edge of Loch Insh, Kincraig. My excitement mounted as we travelled through the valley, with small mountains hovering over us and glimpses of water appearing through the spring greenery on the trees, as rivers and marshes and lochs sparkled invitingly. Loch Insh is really just a wide section of the River Spey, Scotland's third-longest river. We drove into the watersports centre situated right on the shore of this little loch and a large figure stomped over and introduced himself to me as Clive, my new boss and husband of Sally.

I was shown up to my large shared bedroom in the upper floor attic above the restaurant. The window framed a view that looked over the loch and across to the Cairngorm mountain range. It was simply furnished but comfy and it turned out to be ideally situated for us workers as we were able to just fall out of bed at the last minute and stumble down the wooden stairs and to start our shift in the restaurant.

The team of workers were a mix of Scottish, English and Kiwis, all in a similar age group. We bonded really quickly and the camaraderie got us through many long shifts. The centre ran from early morning to late night, hosting school groups for watersports activities with overnight stays in dorms and Bed & Breakfast guests accommodated in log cabins. There was a cafe in the day that switched to an al-la-carte restaurant in the evenings, water sport instruction, and gardens and property to be maintained. As Sally got to know our skills she rostered us on to many different tasks and I ended up enjoying the kitchen shifts helping with menu prep work, entrees, garnishes and plating the dessert orders.

Clive's version of being the boss was so different from my kindly people-focussed London boss Terry. Clive was large in stature and loud, shouty and brisk with his communication. Here was my lesson on invisibility - how to slip out of sight when the boss arrived on the scene. We were fortunate he ran things from a distance, mostly leaving us working as a team to get on with things. There would be sudden frightening shouty appearances of bluster and blunder and then off he would stomp, thinking he had done his bossing.

He was a whisky drinking fisherman and it just took a while for him to gain his confidence in us. His centre still runs to this day and has been running for 50 years. I give credit to the man who had the foresight to start a venture that offered so many experiences to young people, by either learning a new sport, enjoying their leisure time at the centre or as young staff employed by him. Loch Insh Outdoor Centre is now recognised as a place of excellence for sporting instruction and relaxation. Sally was always less scary but quietly educated us in her high expectations of the standard of work output she required and she got that from us.

Unluckily timing my return from a run one day with the arrival of Clive's car pulling up on the drive outside the restaurant, I had nowhere to hide as he appeared around the side of his car, opened the boot and shouted at me to take the fish into the kitchen. In horror I looked down at his catch of an enormous salmon with its glazed death eye looking skyward. "I can't," I stammered. His menacing look at my reluctance to assist was freezing as his dark eyebrows scowled together. "I'm so scared of touching fish," I had to explain.

As a little kid I did love going to the wharf to fish at the harbourside with my Dad and my brother. But for me it was about spending time with Dad and I received no enjoyment in killing another living thing of the world. Dad would bait the line for me and on the odd occasion I caught something, I was so squeamish about touching the writhing scaled body, that Dad would sigh hopelessly at me and unhook the fish.

Solasta

Now, suddenly being forced to do something so
abhorrent to me, I found the confidence to have a voice to
stand up to Clive. True fear must have shown in my eyes as
he gave a disgruntled growl and yelled for me to go and
bring back some large bin liner bags to put the fish in.
Escaping as fast as I could, I ran to the task and appeared
back to find him with the large fish in his arms. "Hold the
bag open girl!" was his order as he tipped the fish in head
first. Holding the bag just off the ground, the weight of the
enormous dead fish body burst straight through the bottom
of the plastic and onto the ground between my feet. Maybe I
screamed like a girl - but I was quickly told to "just get out
of the way!"

Invisibility was my aim for the next few days in case
I had to look that cross man in the eye and see his scorn at
my weakness. Sniffling with a dose of flu on the way, I was
dragging myself through a late evening shift in the kitchen
when he appeared suddenly in the doorway. I buried my head
in the sink of dishes, but heard the head chef singing my
praises of a great night of hard work on a busy turnover of

49

tables and that I had done it all while not feeling great. There was no answer from Clive and I guessed he had stalked off uninterested in anything to do with me. He rattled around at the bar for a while and then a yell came for me to join him. Timidly, I walked out and he handed me a steaming glass full of what he claimed was his quick fix for a dose of flu - a hot toddy containing his favourite whisky.

Bravely sipping the dreaded thing down under his watchful eye to the very last drop, he ordered me off to bed. True to his word I awoke the next morning bright and healthy. I had discovered that within the bluster there was a heart and in it a lesson that we shouldn't take people as the projected selves that they like to show the world most of the time.

Our downtime from shifts was energetic. In this most picturesque and unspoilt landscape we were able to use the centre's kayaks, sailing boats and windsurfers. The loch was bordered with forests and fields and nearby up the road was the old stone Feshiebridge over the River Feshie, under which we swam in the deep green pools and sunbathed on huge flat rocks.

Whilst out jogging, a trail of Scottish midges and horse flies would follow along behind me, allowing for only short breaks to catch my breath before they would launch into an attack. The perfect soundtrack to my highland life played throughout many runs as one of the Kiwi boys I worked with would do his bagpipe practice in one of the fields and his notes would reverberate around the valleys. We walked the hills nearby, crossing over tumbling burns and following the undulations in the land which were carpeted with heather. Other days we stayed lower and hiked trails through the ancient forests where mother nature used all tones of green washes from the colour wheel, painting her form of artistry in the colours of the leaves and shadows of Scots pine, birch, rowan, aspen and junipers. We pedalled the old bikes to cruise the country roads and explore other lochs and rivers further afield and occasionally hired local horses to trek. The horses appeared to hate us and our hopeless horsemanship and headed straight for low branches to try to dismount us.

If we needed to shop we would hitchhike to Kingussie, often being picked up by one of the locals, or we would head off in the opposite direction and catch an occasional bus to the larger township of Aviemore. During the long, long summer days where darkness hardly approached, I found myself many a twilit night sitting on the shore of Loch Insh staring at the water and luxuriating in a feeling of healthiness, enjoying the space, fresh air and appreciating the feeling of being supported by new friends. Stars would eventually blink into appearance in the darkening sky - Scotland was gently doing its healing work on me.

Nearing the end of the summer, under insistent suggestions from our boss Clive, we gathered a large group of us to take a long canoe trip down the River Spey. The watersports instructors had proved themselves to us less experienced paddlers throughout the season and we trusted that they would see us down the rapids with their experience.

We headed out one sunny evening after a shift at work. The midges still skittered around us whilst end-of-day birdsong filled the air. Kitted out in wetsuits and fully safety briefed, we scrambled into our assortment of canoes and with lots of banter paddled out into the middle of the river.

An exhilarating few hours passed navigating firstly the bubbling rapids, growing to rushing rapids, and then dodging rocks through rapids, all the while trying to keep the rapid heartbeat and nerves under control. But a pub was our end destination and there is nothing better at the end of a wild outdoor day than a pub nestled in the local countryside, with brightly lit windows and the offer of a beverage to celebrate the day's achievement. We all arrived safely, damp, tired and happy and, after hauling canoes out and onto the waiting trailers, we single filed straight up to the bar and gave ourselves over to the barman's suggestions.

Clive had fought a long legal battle for us to have been able to have access to the River Spey and achieve this jaunt down the river. In the late 1960s and early 1970s Clive had formed the beginning of his watersports centre and was starting to get grief about canoeists using the waterway and disturbing the fishing. He battled to gain access to the river for recreational water users, other than just fishermen.

The passing into law of the Land Reform (Scotland) Act giving what is now known as the 'right to roam' possibly takes into account his case on water rights in Scotland which became known as the "Spey Canoe Case". Landowners on either side of the river claimed the canoeists from the Centre were disturbing the salmon and making sport fishing less viable. Clive Freshwater was trying to prove that a public right of navigation had been in existence for hundreds of years.

After many years of research and various court cases he had his result. It was established conclusively in the House of Lords that the Spey was a public navigable waterway and it was a crown right that wouldn't run out of time - hence once established, it would remain a right forever. I imagine therefore, that Clive felt mighty proud every time he sent one of his teams of employees down that river to have the experience that he fought long and hard to keep, for the good of all.

Highland autumn signalled its arrival abruptly with a dusting of snow on the mountain tops, an added freshness to the wind and nature started taking a turn on the colour wheel to shades of amber, orange and gold. The work team started winding up and planning began for next adventures. Three of us decided to head South for some continuation of warm weather and after a farewell ceilidh we caught the train down to London to purchase a cheap flight to the city that intriguingly lies in both Europe and Asia - Istanbul.

4

Star And Crescent ☆

A new variant of the Covid-19 virus has been found in the world and highlighted throughout all media. It has officially been given the name Omicron and has been flagged by WHO to be "of concern". Doom and gloom is all the media will focus on, giving us some more fear to feed on. The lesson grows more tense. I find myself switching off from the media more and more and trying to learn a lesson from my cat who now sits nearby at the door of the shed - nap more.

Travelling through Turkey was so immensely enjoyable. The country over obliged itself in its offer of beauty, warmth, adventure and fun. There was an easy friendship between the three of us backpacking together, helped by the fact that we had lived and worked in close quarters with each other in Scotland. We had agreed that we were all doing this trip on the cheap, so we shared rooms in the local Pensions and these were run by a great assortment of characters. At each destination we hopped off a bus to a hustling crowd of accommodation providers and, although we worried at first about which one to pick, we ended up with some wonderful rooms to stay in and learnt to hussle back and find a good price. With haggling finished we would follow our host to the room they had on offer, which was often spacious and airy with wooden floors and large windows flung open to catch a breeze and a Mediterranean view.

It seemed to take only 15 minutes from being a stranger in their homes to becoming part of the family. They would offer such a warmth of greeting and often involve us in meals and gatherings within their families and friends. The family businesses would be presented to us, and we became willing customers of carpet shops, or hungrily partook in cafes and restaurants, and sometimes were taken for lovely drives up hillsides to other restaurants run by extended family members. The longer we stayed somewhere the more invites we got.

Our biggest concern of each day was where the next meal would be coming from. Turkish breakfasts are so worth getting out of bed for. A boiled egg, some black olives, a large piece of feta, tomato slices sprinkled with fresh thyme leaves and a hunk of white bread sometimes with honey or jam, all accompanied by sipping small strong coffees. It was such a charming start for the digestive system just before the real heat of the day arrived.

Immersing myself in some saltwater and with the grit of sand back against my skin from glorious beaches, left me with a massive appreciation for this country. The Mediterranean sea embraced our sun soaked bodies. Fabulous cheap, seasonable food was available everywhere. There were historic monuments and creative carpet makers to visit. We took our time and slowly travelled our way south through the country. We didn't read a newspaper or have any contact with the outside world except when writing the odd postcard to family back in New Zealand. We travelled using a Lonely Planet guidebook, only reading on a day ahead planning which town to possibly make for next.

The coaches we travelled on between towns were new and modern and air conditioned, and the drivers appeared to be ex-fighter pilots with an addiction to speed. Our only mishap was when one bus we were travelling in passed another oncoming bus at mach speed, and they hit each other's wing mirrors off. No stopping to worry about it though; we motored on with gales of laughter from the driver.

A bus boy would be employed to come through the aisle at given intervals to splash 'kolonya' or cologne onto the palms of our hands. Traditionally this sweet-scented aroma is made with fig blossoms, jasmine, rose or citrus ingredients and sprinkled onto the hands of guests at places such as homes, hotels and hospitals. The scent of orange blossom water now takes me straight back to Turkey and its national scent of kolonya. It was a system of hand sanitiser offered in the form of a blessing with the warmth of hospitality from the Turkish people, and had such an intriguing fragrance.

Learning to play backgammon over intensively sweet, yet bitter mint tea was a highlight. I play well to this day and put it down to my training. My teacher had the classic piercing blue eyes of the Turks and had enough spoken English to be initially charming. As I walked by his small table outside a tile-floored coffee shop, he pointed at the empty chair and told me to sit and play. My reply that I didn't know how to play was answered with a disgusted look and I immediately took up the challenge. I seated myself and said, "Teach me". He only knew how to play fast so if I made any move too slowly he would grab my hand and show me by putting my fingers on the pieces to move and we would move them together. He kept ordering tea and we played game after game very intently. When I had finally won a game he paused and put his hands on the side of the board. He looked me in the eye and once again looked disgusted, shoved the board away from him towards me. He got up from his chair and stalked off down the road. Student had excelled and the teacher walked!

We were into our final leg of travelling Turkey and decided to head to Cappadocia - into central Turkey famous for its fairy chimney rock formations and underground cities. We left on a night bus from the busy city of Antalya, excited to be heading to stay in a cave in the town of Goreme. We quickly dozed off, lulled by the movement of the coach, and I awoke in the darkness a few hours later. I had to look and look again with wonder and pinch myself to see if I was really awake. Catching the headlights of the odd passing car I could see what looked like snow falling past the window. I woke my friends and they let out astonished exclamations. We had all packed for summer travelling and no one had snow clothes! We had not appreciated the altitude climb into this region and an early few days of snow was sprinkling the landscape white. There was nothing for it except to put on everything we had in our packs. Three T-Shirts, a fleece, a nylon waterproof jacket and cotton trousers got us through a rather cold two days before the weather turned glorious again. The area is stunning, so exploring on foot is how we kept ourselves warm. We ducked into caved cafes and went underground into the cities exploring these historic places.

Seeing snow was enough to spur us on to somewhere warmer, and one of our group had to return home to the UK and get on with becoming a university student. My leftover friend and I decided to ferry hop our way down to Egypt with its promise of heat. I had explored this country 18 months ago on a group tour and was left in awe, with a burning desire to go back and travel through it at a slower pace.

We caught the first ferry to Rhodes and it was uneventful. We had packed lots of food to build sandwiches from and we had olives and fruit to snack on. A set of playing cards and books entertained us for a while until we chilled on the deck watching the seabirds and the waves. On arrival in Rhodes we popped into the ticket office to investigate getting a ferry to Cyprus over the next couple of days. We were told due to increasingly bad weather that the next ferry in a couple of hours was the last one that would be leaving until the weather cleared, so we decided to buy a ticket and just keep going. We left our bags behind the counter and went for a quick two hour look around Rhodes, stocking up on some more supplies.

On getting back to the port we were told the sea was too choppy for the ferry to come into dock, but we would be taken out by a small boat to catch the ferry anchored off the coast. We hurled our packs over and took a precarious leap between the small craft and a cargo door at the bottom of the ferry to carry on with the journey. At least we didn't have to throw push bikes over the waves as the other two travellers did. We wedged ourselves safely into some seats and had a dippy up and down trip to Cyprus.

Travel weary on our arrival into Limassol, we thought we would overnight and seek out a ferry to Egypt in the coming days. Before looking for accommodation, we checked about ferry tickets, only to be told that there was a strike on and no ferries were running for the foreseeable future. They did have one solution for us, which was to join the weekly cruise boat that was leaving in the next couple of hours on an overnight trip to Alexandria. So once again we forged on and decided to catch this mode of transport. We were offered a ticket for the cheap seats that would allow us a place down in the belly of the ship.

Climbing up the steps of the gangplank and boarding the ship dressed in our shorts and T-shirts and with our backpacks hoisted we felt a little out of place beside nicely dressed tourists arriving to join their cruise. A photographer was stationed at the door to snap a shot of each group beginning their journey. We went into a fit of giggles when we got the offer and posed for a photo that we knew we could not afford to buy. We showed our ticket to a greeting deckhand and they pointed down a hallway leading to some stairs in the opposite direction to where everyone was going. Down and down we went until we reached a deck that was furnished with rows and rows of aeroplane style chairs. We made our way to the front and plonked our bags down, wondering how many others would be taking up these bargain seats.

Star and Crescent

We didn't have to wait long before two guys wearing backpacks came through the door and a cheery "g'day" from one was enough to tell us he was an Aussie. He was long haired and fun loving and we were immediately made to feel friends. The other was blonde and quieter and when he smiled my heart flipped. He introduced himself as Shendon in an English accent. I made for the bathroom and stood in front of the mirror taking a proper look at myself for the first time in a very long time. Preening was happening - there was something about that boy out there that had clicked with me.

We ended up being the only ones travelling in the cheap seats and we had the luxury of having the whole deck to ourselves. The cruise left Cyprus at 2pm and was due to arrive in Egypt at 7am the following morning. We got out a frisbee and played mad games, throwing it up and down the length of the deck through the aeroplane seats and got to know each other. We showered and went up onto the decks above. We pooled money and had enough to buy a drink each from the cocktail bar which we sipped slowly whilst watching the ship's entertainment and the holidaymakers eating.

By the time we were disembarking into a hot early Egyptian morning we were firm friends and had a laugh going through a little cargo shed on the wharf, which was our customs clearance. We made our way into the township and secured rooms in a lovely old Victorian style hotel with metal cage lift and travelled up to our terraced rooms with cooling fans whirring above us on the ceiling.

We met up with the boys again and found a lovely white sandy beach to lay on looking out at the busy shipping lanes while we let ourselves soak up the fact we were now in Egypt.

5

Nothing New Under The Sun ☆

Today New Zealand has claimed to keep up with managing the current pandemic by mandating vaccine passports. We are to prove our vaccination status before entering a premises. I tuck away at the bottom of the garden with no plans to go anywhere today. I am upset that this new law is creating such a division between us within our communities.

Friendships gained whilst travelling have always surprised me with the speed in which you become close buddies. We discussed our various travel plans through Egypt and decided to stick together as a foursome and head off into the sparsely populated Sinai desert region at the top of the country. Sharm el-Sheikh resort promised fabulous snorkelling and it would be my first proper desert destination.

Catching a night bus alongside the Suez Canal I looked out at its busy shipping. Then the bus veered off into the vast sandy terrain where, caught in the bus headlights, I watched clouds of sand blow across the road. Travel definitely teaches trust. Often pushed outside a comfort zone, you are better off trusting in the journey that is unfolding before you instead of worrying about a whole bunch of 'what ifs'. We put our trust in the desert driver and nodded off to the movement of the bus, as all the locals were doing.

The accommodation we found was predominantly little concrete huts with a concrete pad topped with a slim mattress for sleeping and shared bathrooms - rather basic, but this was all we needed. We seemed to hardly need sleep anyway as the dark night skies in the desert are a sight to behold and we wanted to be out amongst the stars. We would lie chatting on beaches feeling miniscule under the twinkling of the heavens. Shooting stars would soar above every minute or so and we silently sent our wishes out into the universe.

One evening found us breaking into a pedal boat park and stirring up the plankton in the dark water as we paddled around in the Red Sea creating magical water bioluminescence that sparkled and fizzed around us. After messing around for quite a while someone did wonder out loud about sharks and we soon paddled back to shore and returned the stolen pedal boats - just in case!

Whenever hunger arrived in our bellies, open air cafes offered enticing small dishes of food to graze on from a shared mezze menu. Being seated on carpets and cushions on the floor at low tables encouraged relaxation and made us linger over our meal breaks. The body slowly reclined more and more as the stomach filled to a satisfying limit. Sandy landscapes lay before us and I was finding that being a child of the beach had adapted me well to desert life. I loved the colours of the sandscapes and the feel of the granules of sand sneaking its way into clothing and buildings and bedding. Sand, it seems, equals happiness for me.

We caught buses around the Sinai peninsula balancing activity with times of chilling. Swimming out and then teetering on the edge of the famous blue hole for snorkelling, we looked out over an enormous drop into a world of startling blue deepening to black water. This felt like stepping out over an abyss. Strangely, having been brought up on a beach I have always held a fear of deep water. I watched my friends swim out over the edge and then take large breaths and dive down as deep as they could go. I dabbled on the side and watched the fishlife darting around the edge.

We made our way to some of the holy sites and climbed the rocky path up Jabal Mousa (Mt Sinai). It was a warm evening and the pilgrimage route was to hike up and spend the night on the top of the mountain, to be ready to watch the sunrise dawning. We were not really equipped for a night in the desert where temperatures plunge. Luckily the locals had taken advantage of this naivety of travellers and for an extortionate price one of them sat at the top of the mountain ready to rent out one of the well worn wool camel blankets from a carefully folded pile. So because we couldn't afford one each, how could a romance *not* start on a mountain, in the desert, awaiting a sunrise, under a shared camel blanket! Shendon and I spent the night under the stars alongside all the other huddled figures and tiredly watched the brilliant sunrise display unfold before us at daybreak.

Still feeling chilled we quickly trotted down the mountain in search of food to break our fast and then to look around the beautifully restful Saint Catherine's Monastery. Stone buildings almost camouflaged into the landscape with the odd tree dotted around offering some shade. Soaring barren rocky mountains lay beyond its walls and it may have been weariness from the lack of sleep, but I wandered around soothed with the sense of peace I felt there.

Time to head back into the main tourist route of Egypt and we caught a bus headed for the capital Cairo. This was my second visit to what is a captivating city and once again it grabbed my interest with every footstep around the crowded streets, markets and world heritage sites.

It turned out that my friend and the Australian were now both after a quicker trip through Egypt. Shendon was on a slower time frame - as was I, and so it was agreed to swap travel buddies and we ended up waving off my friend and the Aussie.

It was suddenly strange to be with this new person alone and there was a little awkwardness in both of us. But Shendon and I got to find the rhythm of the day that suited us both. He was doing a lot of writing and dreamt of becoming an author. He spent much of the day with his nose in his journal and a coffee going cold in front of him in one of the cafes or a hotel restaurant when the weather got too hot. I explored around markets and streets and museums and would go and grab him to drag him off to some of the famous sites. We loved the food and the vibe of Egypt and gave up on the fear of having a relationship and started what we thought of as a holiday romance.

One of my most magical places in the world is the Cairo Museum. Up until I visited this place I had never really been much interested in museums or studied history before. But I spent many hours in this glorious shrine to all things Egyptian. A lovely old guide on my first visit to Egypt had said the words, "in Egypt there is nothing new under the sun," and they have always stuck with me. The Museum pieces are proof that the people here were always ahead of the game, with sophisticated ways of doing every part of life and death. How they treated the death of our physical bodies and even their cats is astonishing with the mummifying process. The human mummies have taken on a little ghoulish persona with various stories and movies over history, but I found the elegant form of the mummified cats to command quite a presence in death just as they do in life.

Fabulous coffee bars abound in Cairo with chairs spilling out onto the street and the scent of caffeine brewing, drawing you in. They were busy, welcoming places and as the enjoyment of coffee goes back to the brotherhood of the Islamic Sufis who drank it during their prayers, it is a lovely salute to this beverage that many of us enjoy around the world. Both business and social meetings took place at such a venue with the odd cat walking in and out and weaving around legs. There is serious care taken over the making of the sweet black strong Arabic coffee or a cheap cup of good standard tea. We shared the space with a majority male clientele of taxi drivers, marketeers, businessmen, youths and the elderly.

Two stone scarab beetles have lived with me in all my homes around the world since these trips to Egypt. The first one is a flat round black stone with a smoothed out base on which is carved the otherworldliness of hieroglyphics. He has minimalist carved details and yet holds quite a presence. It was offered to me by a trader haranguing the tourists at one of the archeological sites and was my first haggled purchase in Egypt. The second is a little turquoise blue intricately carved scarab with the hieroglyphics notched into its wings and also underneath the base. It caught my eye sitting on a bottom shelf of a little market stall and the grime of the market is still ingrained into its carved lines. These small items could slip into my backpack and I have enjoyed these wee pieces of physical Egypt staying with me all this time.

In my previous tour of Egypt we had done an overnight trip down the Nile on the traditional felucca sailboats and it had been a highlight for me. Shendon was happy to do another one with me and this time it was even more fun as we had to find and hire the boatman ourselves, to take us on the two day journey. In the city of Aswan we wandered the riverbank and talked to a couple of felucca boatmen. We soon found one that charmed us enough with his big toothy smile that shone from his crinkled, weathered face and his commitment to bad jokes, so we hired him. He gave us a list of supplies we were to buy at the market for him. He would add this to his basics of flour, rice and couscous, as the deal was that he would also cook all our meals whilst we were onboard.

The traditional wooden sailboat was wide enough for two people to lie across the open deck which is covered in thin foam mattresses and swaddled with carpets and throws and long pillows that stack up around the edges. A tent like cover above allows some protection from the sun. Lying down puts you very close to the water and the green Nile water swirled around and past our vessel. The wind was up and we tacked out immediately into the centre of the wide river to begin our watery journey, tacking to and fro with the one large sail filling and catching the ultimate gusts of wind. Banks of sand towered above us and as we left the city boundary, looking across to the other bank, we could see the narrow strip of land that is cultivated with crops and palm trees using the precious river water. This greenery is a relief from the desert sand backdrop of dunes and in the distance barren rocks and mountains.

We moored at the riverbank for meals that consisted of salad, fish, rice, pita bread and watermelon. The coolness of the wind off the water was enough to relieve the achingly hot Egyptian sunshine and we lay and watched the scenery pass us by. The afternoon drifted by and then some swift sailing happened in the early evening as the wind got up. The gusts were strong enough to break the water's surface, wavelets lapping into the sides of the boat as we tipped at increasingly alarming angles. After the captain had his laugh at us we were put to anchor again to await the wind drop that happens every evening.

We sailed again at sunset watching the pink/purple green wash sweep across the skies. It darkened and a shining moon rose and we were peacefully sailing by moonlight listening to the splash of water and the animal life on the banks. We tied up to the side of the riverbank around 9pm and a bonfire was lit in the sand for us to sit around and enjoy our late dinner. Another felucca arrived, and some locals came across from their mud brick farmhouses, and drums and Nubian musical instruments were played for us. After such a happy day we tucked into our sleeping bags on the deck of our felucca imagining that this was our life always.

Awakening in the morning to a sensation of movement was a bit alarming, until I then realised where I was and that our captain had untied from anchorage and let us drift off with the current whilst prepping our breakfast. A magic start to the day! The wind this second warm day was only wafting, so the first few hours we were mostly flowing with the river current. A small ferry boat bumped up against us at one stage and we tied up to them. The boatmen chatted to each other and lit a cigarette. The town of Kom Ombo was to be our destination and we were almost sad to catch sight of it as we just wanted to keep flowing with the Nile, imagining we were living in the time of the Pharaohs. Shendon, with an ear for languages, was learning a lot of Arabic from the boatman and he wanted to keep his teacher for longer. But disembark we must and so we let our boatman go and find his next clients. Anyway, we were also a bit desperate for a normal toilet as our desert sand hole commodes were something that would take us a bit longer to get used to.

In Luxor we were to witness a horrible undoing of a local man and I have never understood why we were placed within that scene on this given day. Well acclimated to the heat of the Egyptian God of Ra, being beamed from the searing local sun, we hired bikes for a day's outing. We were off to explore over on the West Bank of the Nile the monuments and tombs within the Valley of the Kings and Queens and the most famous of them all, the tomb of Tutankhamun. We joined the local commuters on the early morning public ferry crossing. Rolling our bikes over to the far side we stood holding them up against a barrier on the edge of the barge-like vessel. We were surrounded by the hubbub of jostling local men on their way out to the start of their working day. There was a clearing of lungs with hoiking and coughing and they called out to their friends and lit cigarettes.

As the ferryboat neared the river bank, the barrier came down and the forward movement of the craft would slide the docking ramp straight onto the bank, allowing for a smooth, quick offloading of humans and bikes. Knowing the system too well the local guys didn't bother waiting for the ramp to hit land before the crowd surged forward and began to leap the lessening gap over the water and stride out towards their destinations. The destiny of one particular fellow man was horribly altered this day, right before our eyes.

With a slip of his footing, he fell forward onto the ground and didn't have time to lift himself out of the way from the incoming boat. Its hulk ploughed the landing ramp forward into the bank, cutting straight into this man's leg, severing his foot.

79

Nothing New Under The Sun

The howls of the man, the screaming of the vessel as its engines were thrown into reverse and the ensuing chaos of the frenzied crowd froze us into position. As I gulped for air, my body buckled forward in empathy for the horribly injured man. I was quickly surrounded by local guys, who at once took my bike off me, took me under the arms, used themselves as shields from the vision before me and they gently took me from the boat. We wheeled our bikes some way from the scene and painfully stared at each other, agonising that there was nothing we could do to assist. We didn't have the language or any first aid skills or the knowledge of how these people worked in an emergency.

Suddenly feeling sickened by the crowd of concerned people swarming around me, I angrily waved them off and towards the injured man. I wanted all attention and assistance to be given to this poor fellow. We rode our bikes slowly away from the situation and towards the Valley of the Kings. A man on a scooter soon rode up beside us and waved us to stop and he mimed for us to follow him. We did so, still dazed with what had happened and followed him to what appeared to be his mudbrick home. We didn't really understand what he was offering and he proceeded to invite us inside a corridor which led downwards to an ever deepening underground system of rooms and then he started muttering about hashish.

I paused feeling uncomfortable as I hate caves and tunnels and he grabbed my arm and started physically pulling me along. I quickly said to Shendon "this is getting creepy - lets go!" Luckily he had sensed something strange going on and at the same moment I pulled myself away from the insistent hold on my arm, we turned and ran back up through the dim corridors, out into the blasting sun and hopped on our bikes and rode off as fast as we could.

We took ourselves numbly through the tourist marvels of the tombs and spent most of the day there, as we were so nervous about catching the ferry back. We asked around and found we could catch the more expensive tourist boat back across the Nile at the end of the afternoon. We were then very ready to find a bar, to order a stiff drink and to try and process the happenings of the crazy day.

Our month journeying in Egypt had seen the relationship between Shendon and myself grow into a comfortable friendship. As we travelled together we supported each other through all the new experiences thrown at us, had enough common interests to debate and mull over, and through our daily changing circumstances we were starting to understand how each of us liked to take on the world. Shendon's travel time was up though and he booked a flight back to England. I still had savings to spend and I wanted to carry on travelling for a little while longer before heading back to the UK, so I decided to catch a long bus ride off to Israel and find a Kibbutz or Moshav to work on.

It was a sad parting. Catching an early morning bus from Cairo, I moped the whole journey to Israel. Shendon hadn't given me too much hope that our relationship would continue on beyond a holiday romance and I stewed over this seeming lack of commitment. I had feelings for him which had cemented in over the month we had travelled together and I wanted the relationship to continue. A time apart may be good for him to realise what he missed and we had agreed to stay in contact while I was still travelling.

6

Magen David (Star of David) ☆

The Omicron variant of Covid-19 has leaked through our tight border controls and has set about in the community. Our regulations on how we are to live our lives have quickly been changed again and we have been given a new traffic light system with different guidelines for restrictions with self isolation. The whole of New Zealand is now at the highest level of red where mask use and vaccine passport is mandatory most places and crowd sizes are kept small with social distancing in place. We are touted numbers everyday - being the predictive cases in line with what other countries have experienced. The numbers are large. It's hard to remain untriggered by the thought of so much illness about to swamp us. Absolutely nowhere have I heard mention of some self care and self responsibility of our immune system and a possibility of the power of positive thinking.

Magen David

I had chosen a seat near the back of the bus, succumbing to a bum-numbing 12 hour journey once again through the Sinai Desert to Israel, and let my thoughts wander back reflecting on the great time I had just had for the last month. There was a mournful pang of endings and the feeling of emptiness inside me, suddenly travelling alone.

I slept fitfully and when we eventually stopped at the border it was in this slightly depressed mood that I came up against the ugly Israeli customs regime. I had to get myself quickly out of the funk I had got myself into to be able to try to interpret what the rather threatening armed guards were asking of me. We had to disembark from the bus and stumble half asleep through various wired off areas with questions being barked at us from a series of basic caged windowed huts. We made our way slowly into a concrete building and my mumbled replies finally saw the right stamp banged into my passport and we were pushed through the far door and officially into Israel.

My buddy was no longer around to send a glance over to in a tricky situation to lighten the mood and I missed him already. I had to appear brave and look as though I knew what I was doing so as not to upset the customs police. It was a jolt from the nice hospitable time I had just had in Egypt.

Customs cleared, the bus continued on to Tel Aviv where I collapsed for a night at a backpackers. I didn't feel completely comfortable in this city and although I had initially thought to tour a bit of Israel, I decided I needed a little more knowledge of travelling this country and went straight to a recruitment agency to sign up for work at one of the communities. A Moshav at the bottom of Israel at the south end of the Dead Sea was on the lookout for produce pickers and it sounded remote enough to once again have an interesting address. I signed up, found a bus and headed for Moshav Neot HaKikar whose boundary bordered Jordan.

Jumping down from the bus and being blasted by the hot sandy air, I entered the Moshav gate and made my way into the compound. Small basic huts were dotted around slightly larger dwellings with wide dust roads. With some assistance from a small child I found my way to the house of the farmer I would be working for. He was a short man who was also short on English. He showed me what was to be my room in one of the compact four bedroomed huts and told me to await the return of my fellow workers for their lunch break and then to go out to the fields with them when they did the afternoon shift.

The huts had no glass in the windows due to the hot climate, but screens against flies and mozzies were tacked up. The fields of dusty green produce and long rows of date palms stretched out from the dwellings and I wondered what my working day was going to look like.

Three suntanned people wearing cut off jeans and old Tshirts soon appeared and welcomed me warmly into the fold of the house - happy to have another worker to lighten their load. They were at the end of the melon picking season and after feeding me some lunch we plonked hats on our heads and headed out into the sun for an afternoon working our way, bent over, down the lines and lines of melon vines cutting the ripe fruit off with a knife. The delicious aromatic creamy white flesh of a perfectly ripe juicy melon was so refreshing in the heat and we sneakily ate quite a few. My new friends gleefully told me horror stories of the farmer whom we were working for, so sneakily is how we had to eat - of course making it taste so much better.

The Moshav nestled into the border plains before they rose into the mountains of Jordan. By hopping over the fence at the back of the melon fields we could claim to tick another country off our bucket lists by stepping a foot into Jordan. Sonic booms regularly sent shock waves through us as military aircraft flew around this area reaching past the speed of sound. The nearby Army base gave us a good source of transport, offering us rides when we were out hitchhiking around the local area.

After melons, we then spent the next few weeks picking tomatoes from their spicey odorous bushes. They had been left to grow naturally into a sprawling knotted mess of stems. Our boss would occasionally pass by the fields and yell, "Pick faster, pick faster!", causing us to pause and pick slower.

Magen David

We were allowed to shelter in the barn when the occasional downpour of rain came through and rather than luxuriate in some rest time, we set up a gym style circuit workout regime using various tools and equipment we found in the building. A snowy heart faced barn owl sat in the rafters deigning to open one eye to stare down at us every so often, checking up on the intrusive interruptions to its daylight sleep hours.

We earned only a little cash each week and saved money by living on basic food. One of our housemates had a Scicillian parentage and his wonderful Mamma had taught him pasta making skills. Very cheaply with flour and water he would roll out vast swathes of pasta sheets, draping them off the sides of the table to help stretch the dough to the correct thinness and then chop it into long strands for our meals. Fresh pasta with stolen tomatoes and the odd avocado and a rock melon for dessert were a firm favourite.

But once again the snow found me! We awoke freezing one morning, to look out to the nearby hills of Jordan to see them covered in some rare snow. We rushed to the shed that held bags of old clothing left over from past workers and donned three pairs of jeans in varying sizes to try to get some warmth to go out to the fields. Everyone clambered for the tractor driving duties on those few days of coolness. The cold wind swept through our glassless house and I handed in my notice and prepared to leave the job.

I made my way back to Tel Aviv, forming a plan to do a trip to Jerusalem, but once again the gloom of that city, the harshness of the land and the toughness of the people left me homesick for the United Kingdom. I packed it in, bought a ticket on the next flight to England and then had to undergo some severe checks at the airport as they were suspicious of me buying a plane ticket and leaving all on the same day.

I just made it as the last person onto the plane and aircraft doors were slammed behind me. I scooted into my seat avoiding the annoyed looks of fellow passengers who had been waiting and looked out the aircraft window saying a silent shalom to Israel.

7

Falling Star ☆

A special press report today presented by the New Zealand Prime Minister, Jacinda Adern announced that they want us all boosted with another shot of vaccine. They have shortened the time between our second vaccine and the new booster to stab us again as quickly as they can. And yet I now have first hand experience of vaccine harm and become less enticed by the saga they want us to play along with. We do demand and love a quick fix as the human race and I guess we have asked for this. Do I foresee booster shots becoming mandated and life restrictions even harder - I hope not.

Couchsurfing at the old biscuit address flat on Shrewsbury Mews gave me a bed for a week and I rang Terry to see if there was a job going back in Drury Lane. "Absolutely," he shouted down the line, "we need you as soon as you can start!" and so I slipped back into my former role. The business had gone from strength to strength with new exciting clients coming on board. I was earning decent money again and with snowflakes descending onto London pavements, I finally purchased an English trenchcoat and my first ever scarf to keep my bones feeling warm and cosy, whatever the weather.

From a coinbox I rang Shendon and he agreed to come to London to meet up, for what was in my mind a date. A loud lively Mexican bar seemed a good neutral spot to catch up and after some polite conversation we soon found our old travel friendship coming to the fore. Crunching on nacho chips and sipping refreshing margaritas, he told me he had moved back in with his parents on the south coast of England and was thinking of returning to his former work in insurance, as his travelling had left his finances a bit diminished. The night lived up to my expectations and he seemed pretty happy to see me again. I was flat hunting and we decided he would come back to visit when I had settled somewhere.

Falling Star

After following a few leads for flats that didn't entice me to stay, I went to look at a bedsit in Leytonstone near the end of the central line tube out in East London. A slim lady answered the door and in her lilting Irish accent asked me in. She showed me along the dark hallway of her Victorian house and up two flights of stairs to the loft which was roomy enough for a bed, couch, tv and a set of drawers. A wee kitchenette in an alcove under a dormer window had a sink, hotplate and fridge. The dormer window on the other side of the room was the wardrobe and storage space. The bathroom on the floor below was shared with her and sometimes one other border she took in the house. I liked her and the warm granny feel to her house which was heavily doily decorated and decided a room on my own at age 25 would be a nice change, so I took up her rental. She ended up being a gracious little landlady and she had no problem with Shendon coming to visit on the weekend.

Soon enough I got the official seal of approval from him when I was invited down to stay with him for a weekend and to meet his family. Catching the busy train south after work on a Friday evening, he met me at the station and took me for a drink at a local pub to brave me up for the meeting. They were a welcoming family and I needn't have worried and I ended up with no qualms about going back to visit regularly on alternate weekends.

It wasn't long before Shendon and I agreed that we still wanted to make travel a reality again and we decided to buckle down for a year, save everything we could and then make our way around the world ending up back in my country of origin, New Zealand. Travel was our common goal and we knew we backpacked well together.

My work life in London was busy, varied and satisfying. We had marketing to do for The Royal Ballet as they were recording their work onto DVDs which was the new technology being introduced to the world to take over from the old VCR. We were organising the PR for an exhibition in Birmingham for some Russian cold war technology now being put to new use. I had my work, I had my boyfriend and I had travel plans. Everything seemed to be lining up as I wanted.

Falling Star

Shendon had initially blown somewhat hot and cold in regard to how serious our relationship was to be. But I had worked my charming magic and felt he had come around to a position of acceptance which was somewhat in agreement with me, that we were onto something here. Unfortunately, with his decision to acknowledge that we had become a serious couple, it now seemed that I became his claim. He became jealous of anyone, or in fact anything, that took my attention away from him. It took me a long while to fathom the behaviour pattern - to realise that some of the things I told him about, that I had done during my week in London, would throw him into a state of moodiness. I found myself not exactly lying to him, but definitely leaving out some of the details of the way I had spent my time apart from him.

He was clever and made the behaviour seem as if it was a compliment to me. I had long wanted him to be more serious about our feelings for each other. This new protective show he upheld about our time together allowed me to see he had reached something of a commitment to our relationship. Agonisingly, it then became too dedicated from his side, as he commanded that my full attention be granted solely to him. And yet alongside these subtle demands from me, he was usually completely charming, easily covering up the slightly obsessive strands to his personality.

We very rarely went out with any of his other friends. When I was down visiting for the weekend he would want the time to be exclusively for us. Like a falling star hurtling to Earth, the bright light we at first shone as a couple was alas destined to disintegrate.

And yet we had grown even closer and helped each other through a few health blips. Having got involved with his family life, I decided the relationship was worth working on and keeping up. I learned to walk on eggshells through the bad bits and as we mostly had a long distance relationship, only seeing each other on weekends, it was easy enough to get on a train back to London at the end of a weekend and forgive him another of his jealous ranting episodes.

Claude came back into the mix with his work bringing him regularly to the office and once again he became a soothing presence in my life. He was the kind, uncomplicated friend who took the time to get to know me. I was invited to a few social parties with work colleagues and Claude would often be there and we would magnetise to each other's side and enjoy a drink and a catch up. He was always charming, polite and witty and although I tried not to, at times I did compare him to Shendon. Claude didn't let on much about his private life, but I didn't get a feeling there was anyone taking up too much of his time and I knew he lived alone.

Shendon and I saved hard and began to purchase pieces of equipment and gear that we would need on our world tour. We had started spending lots of our weekends on the south coast of England, walking many of the trails we could get to from his house. A vigorous walk in the countryside ending up at a pub fireside or garden bar, depending on the season, was enough to get me through another week in the city.

We had added trekking in Nepal as one of our destinations on the planned world tour. We needed good

96

quality tramping boots and one weekend we headed an hour away into the small market town of Arundel to a well known outdoor shop that stocked some. We also bought the latest sleeping bag that scrunched down really small into its little bag and a cooker and a billy pan.

The time of finishing up our jobs was nearing and we felt excited to get on the road again, but also a little nervous to be leaving our comfortable well fed city lives. A larger farewell party was performed for me by Franklin Associates, as this time it was unknown if I would return. We all went to lunch at Sarastro, the wonderful new Mediterranean restaurant further down Drury Lane. The party then carried on back at the office where favourite clients turned up to join in and I was given the big send off.

During the celebrations Claude pulled me aside at one stage and said, "Happy travels, keep in touch and if you are not married by the time you are 30 then I'll marry you myself." He had said this to me a few times over the year we had worked together, in what I had thought was flirting jest. Yet this time there was a deeper look in his brown eyes and as he leaned forward and kissed me on the cheek, I felt a zing of emotion happen for a fraction of a second, feeling a connection or promise had been made, which made the moment more meaningful and memorable. Not knowing how else to react, I laughed his comment off and in reality thought, here I was at 25 years old - it would be an extremely nutty thing to do if it ever came to it in five years time.

My life again fitted into one bag and a lightness of being came over me, now owning only a few possessions. Shendon and I boarded our first plane and began our six month voyage across continents, planning on taking our time in the vastness of India, with all the intrepidness it teaches a Western traveller.

8

Tara - Star (Sanskrit) ☆

Light summer rain is pattering down outside and through the open door of the garden/writing shed I hear the beautiful song of our native bellbird. Soulful bells are their tune and I only hear them close to the house on rainy days, reminding us of the joy in rain. My brother has received notification of Omicron in his workplace, my sister-in-law sends me a photo of the big hole in her arm having just received her booster shot, and my son, who had an adverse reaction to his first vaccine, is booked to have his second today. Bellbird, please bless this day.

Any reading and study I had done on this far off place had obviously been romanticised into my system by my reading of The Far Pavilions by M.M.Kaye. Our arrival into Bombay was rocky and turbulent as the plane did an ear popping nose dive steeply towards the runway through monsoon clouds. The monsoon had delayed its arrival, seemingly awaiting our entry into the country for even more added excitement and challenge. As we exited through the dark brooding turbulent clouds, our view out of the plane window before touchdown was an immense area of cobbled together slum housing made of sacking, bamboo and plastic. It was a bleak picture to look out on.

The humidity hit us on leaving the aircraft and the smell of raw humanity hung in the air, ready to be inhaled with every breath. I had never truly experienced culture shock until those first few days in India where the clash between the way my life had been lived up until this time, compared to this country, smacked me in the face at every footstep. India, like the negatives you receive with your pack of printed photos, appeared at first to be all about the shadows starring as the highlights and the pretty bits are pushed back to be hidden in the dark.

The first few weeks were spent trying to acclimatise to the intense monsoon humidity whilst doing what should have been simple tasks like purchasing bottled water and finding something to eat. People seemed to live down at feet level, sleeping on a piece of cloth on the pavements. Tripping over people living on the street as we walked along, we would glance down and find a pot with an alarming cobra rearing its head out of the lid belonging to a snake charmer. Bottled water was notoriously just refilled from the town supply and it was hard to work out where the dubious bottles were being sold, as it all looked dubious to our new naive eyes. We had arrived armed with iodine though to add to the bottles for any time we thought we had suspect water.

Hunger won over and we started our journey into Indian restaurants and began to enjoy the cheap local dishes done with a simple limited vegetable range. The ambiance at these eateries was gloomy. To keep the air conditioned air wafting over the clientele (on the odd occasion that the air conditioning unit worked between power cuts), the rooms were heavily curtained and dark. We wondered about the lack of fresh vegetables and fruit on our trip, but imagined the monsoon weather had a part to play in the limited supplies. Alas, our stomachs soon rebelled at curries for every meal, and doses of sickness regularly stopped us in our tracks, sometimes holed up in better locations than others.

Awakening to another hot morning from a restless sleep with multiple trips to the bathroom, Shendon yelped as he looked at his arms. Huge welts had appeared and as he investigated further he found them all over himself. The itching began and with a quick read through our guidebook we suspected we now shared the bed with bed bugs! To be bedridden with bed bugs eating you is just not fun and doesn't improve when the solution to kill bed bugs is a good spray with petrol on the mattress.

Getting around India is fascinating and fun to get involved with if you are not in a hurry. We bought the huge paperback annual of the train system and timetables, and after much study we found that we became quite good at working out times of trains and routes we could take. It took away some of the queuing at train stations trying to ask someone for the information. With a route in mind, we elbowed our way to kiosks with everyone else, respecting the space of the odd sacred cow standing around, to purchase our tickets. We even became happy to lie on our packs on platforms of train stations awaiting early or late trains that ran to a relatively delayed time.

Posting a parcel home was a well oiled system involving many postal people, each with a job to do. Someone cut cloth and sewed the parcel together, another person waxed the seams, another tied it up with white string, another did customs forms, another glued the mass of stamps required to post across the world. Sending packages of our books we had finished and the odd souvenir back home was rather enjoyable as it was a soothing process to stand under a large fan in the special part of the post office, cooling ourselves off while they happily did their tasks. The GPO impressed us as we picked up our letters from family and then left forwarding Poste Restante addresses for our next destinations in case we had missed any and we always had letters efficiently forwarded on to us.

Traffic on the roads was always terrifying to me and the run in we had with angry rickshaw wallahs in our early days put me off. Seated in the narrow backseat of our rickshaw behind the driver who had been hurtling us around in an erratic manner, he banged into contact with a vehicle on our side. It had made a loud noise, bumped us and given us a fright, but had done no great damage. The driver had come to a stop in the heavy traffic with his rickshaw wedged between a bus and a truck when he was suddenly set upon by upset people whom he had hit. As it started to become violent, we decided to make a hasty exit and climbed out of our rickshaw through a small gap in the bars. Luckily the traffic remained at a stand still for us to be able to get across lanes to the road edge. We paid the driver off once his altercation was finished as I didn't have the courage to get back in his rickshaw.

Some long bus journeys we were on took as many as five stops to change tyres from punctures and blow outs. Shendon was often out with his torch on the night trips as they didn't seem to be prepared with one for what seemed such a common occurrence. They would flag down oncoming trucks and buses and a whole range of tyre swapping would take place and eventually we would rattle off into the night again.

But slowly we settled into our way of life on the road again and became familiar with the correct way to buy tickets at rail stations; to not believe every rickshaw driver's first price; or to believe the touts that told us that somewhere we wanted to go was closed or fallen down and he knew a better place - obviously taking us to his friend or family to wiggle our rupees out of us. As we wisened up we tried to beat their systems, but the touts were desperate for some income and followed us relentlessly, which I found a shame as our first impression of any new town was always of these conniving characters.

Finding a spot to set our packs down on the trains and taking a seat, we may as well have been purple dinosaurs, wearing tiaras and juggling ice cubes. The open stares we received from the whole carriage of people was discomforting. We paid higher prices for first class tickets to have a seat in a less populated compartment, often sharing with a whole family squished on to one bench seat. But still the fascination with our strangeness won over and they eyeballed any movement we made. Shendon's sun bleached white blonde hair offered some uniqueness to their day and as we were hardly meeting any other travellers around at this time I guess we did stand out to the locals.

The mass of humanity living in monsoon conditions makes for a mud-splattered environment and yet the most beautiful coloured saris would sparkle out of the gloom as ladies carried pots of water on their heads with a small child tucked in on the hip. Children heading to school would wear immaculate uniforms. A long bearded figure having finished cutting grass with his buffalo-drawn lawn mower stood leant up against a tree smoking a cigarette, whilst his buffalo tucked into the clippings of his labour. Glimpses of beauty shone out of each dripping heated day.

Daylight in the Indian continent has a pinkish tinge to it and arriving into the city of Jaipur where the old buildings are also coloured pink gave the town a dreamlike quality. We photographed many of the settings hoping to capture some of the pearlescent feel to the days. The monsoon clouds finally grew heavy enough to pour out their drops and deluge the roads in ankle deep water. Here was the benefit of owning tramping boots, and we felt safer striding through unseen debris of small rivers in our new boots. Many camels were the animal of choice in Rajasthan, put to the hard work of hauling loads. Riding a rickshaw amongst long camel legs is bemusing. Anybody is out for a rupee in this land and so as the monsoon water rose to knee high, we stayed back at our accommodation and paid a willing man to cross the road to purchase a large bottle of beer for an evening drink.

Working our way to the South of India over six weeks, the intrepidness of it all never gave a break. Bombarded with people wanting to shine our shoes, give us a massage, take us somewhere, sell us a cigarette and beg us to give them money, any time we stepped out of our accommodation was draining. We remained standing out as the odd strangers far from our homelands. As Shendon's birthday loomed, we realised that we could give ourselves a break from the challenges of India by flying to the Maldives and taking a holiday to celebrate.

Finding the cheapest all inclusive island package on Lohifushi, located in the North Male Atoll, we booked to stay in a small thatched beach hut. Our shrunken stomachs were put to the test as we tried to feed ourselves the regular meals on offer which graced loaded tables with lots of fresh fruit and vegetables. We loafed around in the calm sea and picked up tiny shells off the white coral sand beaches while watching big skies with weather squalls come and go, as we were still on the edge of the monsoon influence.

Speeding along in a boat, with flying fish leaping in our wake as it took us back to the atoll on which just the airport runs the full length of the island, our excitement built - we were off once again to catch our next flight, this time to Sri Lanka. Two weeks of Sri Lankan life was also good for our travel weary bodies. Apart from the small minibuses, where nearly 50 people would crush into them for a claustrophobic ride, most of our experiences were calm. The beaches were barraged with tremendous waves from the monsoon systems passing through, but they were still beautiful. Accommodations were built nearby to take advantage of this beauty and we stayed close to the sand dunes and spent warm nights out star gazing.

Through luck we had timed our visit to Sri Lanka to coincide with the famous Perahera Elephant festival and caught the train up to the high country, looking out open air barred windows to rice paddies, then through the prolific growth of jungle rainforest flora and fauna to the town of Kandy, atop a plateau surrounded by mountains. As we wandered around the town in the afternoon we spotted elephants being scrubbed down with coconut husks and drinking from the town fountain, being made ready for their nighttime parade performance.

Our tourist seats were tiered stands at the edge of the street at the start of the event, and we arrived early to find our seats and watch the crowds of people start to gather and unpack picnics while waiting for the festivities. Salesmen offered balloons, whistles and pineapples to the children of the families, adding to their obvious excitement. As darkness approached the twinkling lights sparkled into life, highlighting every tree, temple and building in the vicinity.

Tara

A huge skyrocket firework started the parade of whip crackers, flaming fire throwers, drummers and dancers, and then came the main feature: the 95 elephants adorned in huge embroidered covers. They were also hung with lights which were draped over their heads and down their trunks powered by large batteries perched beside the riders. Their large tusks were close to us, and the sparks from the fire torches blew around us, and the noise was chaotic yet primal, but for two hours we were transported to some other world.

I now question the welfare of the elephants through this event and in fact I have since read of elephant attacks occurring at the parade, so the beasts are sending a message I hope. But the area is famous for its use of elephants and the local orphanages for baby elephants are part of the local industry for income.

Flying back into Southern India we then journeyed by train back up through the vast country to arrive in Varanasi two months later. The site of the holy Ganges was something we had looked forward to experiencing. The juxtaposition of life and death played out daily beside this river was so different to my western eyes, where death is a subject which is not talked about much until it shockingly confronts you when it happens to a loved one amongst your circle of contacts. Here on the Ganges life happened alongside death, joy of the holy site was experienced alongside grief at the death of a fellow human.

Whilst men and women at the bathing ghats stepped into the river up to their waists to wash and brush their teeth, goats and dogs wandered on the stairs and a crowd gathered around a guy with dancing monkeys. A little further down the river bodies of the dead were burnt within large piles of wood on the burning ghats. Those who could not afford such a luxury - children, holymen, smallpox victims, untouchables and the very poor who aren't cremated - were instead wrapped in white cloth and delivered straight into the river. Bloated animal carcasses washed past in the dark brown brooding swiftness of the current of a river filled with monsoon runoff. On a short boat trip in an old canoe we hired where three oarsmen were struggling with the current, I asked them whether people didn't get sick brushing their teeth and rinsing out their mouths in this water. "Of course not," one replied, "it's holy water." I bravely dipped my fingertips in and requested a blessing.

The week before our time here in Varanasi, I had found out from a telephone call to Shendon's parents that my grandfather had recently died. Saddened by the news I wasn't to see him again and the fact I wasn't able to give him a send off, I sat on the steps of the holy river early one morning just before dawn and wondered what my Irish born Grandpa would have thought of the scene before me. A little boy approached selling tealight candles balanced on a large leaf within a bed of flower petals to float down the river. I purchased one and set it into the river watching as it was grabbed by the current and whisked away down river. I was wishing farewell to my Grandpa from planet earth and asking his forgiveness for not being physically present when he passed. A red ball arose from the horizon and once again swamped the land in pink light as the sun rose up to begin another day.

Tara

Darjeeling became our last stop in India before heading into Nepal to begin our trekking. The famous narrow gauge steam train, fondly referred to as the toy train, was our preferred mode of transport up into the mountains to reach Darjeeling and we chugged off at 8am from the town of New Jaipurguri down on the plains. The two passenger carriages and a luggage carriage hooked to the steam engine were painted bright blue and had open sides allowing for the full steam experience as the hot coal ash blew in over us and soot gently settled over everything.

Tracks for the train followed the roadside and crossed over the road 132 times with no traffic signals or barrier warnings. I eyed up blind corners on the road trying to listen for trucks and traffic coming around to find us in the middle of the road, but we safely avoided all traffic. The track wound around up the mountainside looping back on itself, with switchbacks slowing the progress as the train stopped, then reversed back up the next track, to then move forward again. We glimpsed down into huge valleys and out across into clouds forming on the mountains.

Seven hours was the journey time to Darjeeling but at 2pm, after five hours of toiling up the mountains, we fell off the rails. Crawling along at a slow pace the train stopped and everyone left their seats and got off. We hopped off too and saw the carriage in front of us had its front wheels off the line. Here was my first experience of a derailment and we hadn't even realised what was going on. The guard informed us a replacement would come and take over and it would take three hours to get there. A large pole had arrived from somewhere and many men had propped it under the carriage and were hanging off the end of it trying to lever the carriage back onto the rails. We quickly reached in and grabbed our packs out, having visions of the whole train toppling over the edge of the cliff we were on.

Not wanting to wait for another three hours we managed to flag down a bus coming up the hill and completed our journey up into the clouds and rain to arrive at the bottom of the town of Darjeeling. It is built in a series of steep streets winding up a mountainside, so not much traffic drives the roads except for the odd jeep. It was nice to arrive

114

at a traffic free place and we hefted up our packs and trekked up to the top of town. New faces were looking at us now, as the town is full of Nepalese and Tibetan people living here.

Olde Main Bellevue Heritage Hotel was our chosen accommodation and it sat high above town, slightly forlorn looking, from the British-Raj days, but the atmosphere at the slightly rickety place was delightful, surrounded by wood panelling and shiny wooden floors. The outlook was out to mountains of the Himalayas on one side and down through the town square of Darjeeling on the other. An enclosed long wooden terrace with tables and chairs dotted along under large windows gave us shelter from the cool mountain breeze and we were regularly served tea there by the Tibetan lady who ran the place. It was startling to feel cold after all the heat we had been through in the past four months.

Tea is what this area of West Bengal is famous for and the neatly handpicked waist high brilliant green bushes stretch through large swathes of undulating valleys and hillsides. Pickers move through deftly plucking off the tips of the new growth and throw them into baskets slung on their backs, supported by wide bands on their heads.

Crossing the wooden floor of our room on getting out of bed one morning, I eased open the window to let some morning air enter and feeling the coolness, I leapt back into bed. Creeping in over the window sill came the wisps of a cloud. It was so beautiful to be so fully surrounded by clouds that they even wafted into your room. The high altitude tea plantations are so often softly caressed by clouds and I surmise one of the secrets in the taste of a great cup of Darjeeling tea is this hug they receive from the ethers. Cheers to drinking a cup of cloud tea!

9

Stars for Miles ☆

As predicted our case numbers of the Omicron Covid 19 pandemic are growing steadily in New Zealand and most regions have now been exposed. Protestors have created a tent city outside parliament in our capital Wellington against the current mandated regulations which have forced people out of jobs and restricted their movements. This summer morning I had a dip in the ocean. The sun beating down painting the sea water with twinkling lights highlighting several gulls bobbing on waves just out from me. Salt water supports me both physically and emotionally.

'Namaste' - the divine in me recognises the divine in you, is used when greeting another in Nepal. Use of this, now universally recognised, placement of the hands in the prayer position, thumbs gently resting on your chest at heart level, is a profound way to acknowledge the presence of someone passing you by on the track high up on a mountain pass. This welcome was new to me and I loved it immediately and have used it many times in my life to this day. We had organised our trekking passports and were making our way around the Annapurna Sanctuary trek with its highest point at the Annapurna Base Camp for climbing, at 4130 metres high.

Once again the monsoon was late. Our mornings out on the trail were clear and crisp but the afternoons would become shrouded in cool clouds as the weather rolled over the mountains and into the valleys. We adjusted to doing early morning starts aiming to get the best views of the day. The mid afternoon would find us looking for a spot to stop for the day in a remote village. We would find a teahouse to stay in for the evening and be sipping hot black tea by the time the clouds rolled in. A small room with a couple of basic beds in it and a meal with the host family was what you paid for at each stop.

A long drop toilet with woven grass walls was the bathroom and the higher up the mountains you trekked the more expensive it was to order a bucket of hot water, if you wanted one to wash in. The fuel for the fires to heat this water had to be trekked in and so the expense was relevant to the distance covered. We chose just to splash some cold water around from streams we passed on the tracks each day, cooling my wrists and filling up my cap with the fresh water to plop it back on my head and let the cold droplets invigorate me.

My 26th birthday morning was heralded in by the meeting of two water buffalo ambling towards us on the track through a thick rhododendron forest. We stepped to one side and they snuffled their wet grey noses at us and plodded on through, claiming their well deserved ownership of the trail. Once we had chosen our teahouse in a small settlement we noticed how cool it was getting as we reached higher altitudes and nearer the snow each day. I decided to shout myself a birthday bucket of hot water and quickly sluiced it over my grubby body before it cooled down. It was one of the most memorable birthday baths of my life.

Older couples undergoing the trek had secured sherpas to carry their packs for them. The sherpas threw the western style packs into the large baskets they carried on their heads and with big hearty smiles they moved steadily up tracks, often just wearing jandals on their feet. At each stop for the evening we would find the same people stopping for the day and we got to know a few of them along with their sherpas. The sherpas took us under their wings and would often hand us a welcome cup of hot tea as we trekked into an area, just because they had a billy on the boil.

Remote mountain communities obviously used the trekkers for income and offered their hospitality by cooking extra food to eat at their tables. It was much better to eat the food that they cooked for their families and ever since my trekking adventure, lentil dhal has become one of my comfort foods. I figure if it can get me up a mountain track every day, it has to be good for you. The families would also offer western delights to those trekkers who would despair of eating anything foreign, but you took the risk of a bowl of weevils included in your cornflakes!

Stars for Miles

One of the revered mountains in the Annapurna range is Machapuchare, meaning fish tailed mountain. It's a beautiful mountain with steep sides that surge upward into the sky in the silhouette of a fish tail. It is believed to be sacred as one of the homes of Lord Shiva and views to this goal taunt you the whole route. You slowly make your way towards the mountain to stay a night at its base camp before climbing a steep track up to the Annapurna base camp and the highest point of the trek.

We had set our alarms for a 4am start but already at such a high altitude we awoke gasping many times in the night, our bodies thinking we were out of air. We headed out into the blue black finish of the nighttime darkness, pierced through by starlight and a large moon, and were surprised at how well we could make out the track. We took our time and made a slow ascent to base camp with early morning light pinking the top of Annapurna. Our sherpa friends grinned at our arrival to camp and we were handed a hot cuppa whilst we sat gasping for air overlooking a massive glacier, enjoying the immense scenery and celebrating being alive.

This was the highest altitude I had ever achieved, it was extra special to me as proof of overcoming adversity. In the 18 months leading up to this travel adventure I had twice been put into hospital in London, from a spontaneous pneumothorax. This sudden onset of a partially collapsed lung for no apparent reason is more common in adolescent, thin, tall males. Nobody could give any explanation as to why this had happened to me. Luckily when I was put in a hospital bed for a painful four days - each time monitored and x-rayed - my lung never got beyond a 30% collapse so no intervention of needles into my chest wall was required.

My body healed itself, but I was then warned numerous times that one of my risk factors would be going to altitude. I was determined not to let this become a fear that limited anything I chose to do in life. When I felt strongly that I wanted to trek in Nepal, this became a lesson to me to listen and follow my intuition. I had done the route in a slower time, allowing my body to adjust to the height each day. Mentally, I chose to not bring with me a fear of 'what if' and instead turned it into an affirmative 'I wonder'.

On our way back down the track, after a few days we started meeting people just heading out on their first few days of trekking. The oddity of the scent of clean bodies coming towards us made us turn our noses up. The chemical smell of toothpaste and shampoo and deodorant wafted up the track before the people and it didn't feel right. What we have learned to believe is the smell of cleanliness was now feeling to us an affront to nature. Goodness knows what our rank earthy smell was to them as we passed by. Namaste.

Culture shock in reverse hit us on arrival into the sanitised, shiny modern city of Singapore. Fast moving traffic was actually following the traffic rules and regulations, unlittered streets with wide smooth pavements, large shopping malls, and food in abundance. But all this came at a cost to our travel budget, so we moved on more quickly now catching trains and buses through Singapore, Malaysia and crossed over into Thailand.

New cultures were our teachers as we immersed ourselves in new foods and tried to embrace all new experiences making our lives on the move feel so rich. There were still many irksome travel hiccups and travel sickness woes on the road, but we took turns to rally each other on and once again stuck together as travel buddies, most days enjoying the sharing of our chosen way of being.

Yet, for me, there was an underlying disquiet that ran parallel to our experiences of being on the road. I now also had the time for reflection and I had begun looking back over the past year and realising that I had become craftily netted by this man. The more time I spent in this relationship with Shendon the more the net was slowly being hauled in and tightened, allowing for less and less freedom of thought and movement.

He had now committed to the two of us having a partnership to the detriment of me being able to be myself. I was patterning my behaviour to please him, so as not to put him in a mood. I felt like I was losing me in the equation and I wasn't sure that this was how a healthy relationship should work. The only thing I could do was start to close down my feelings for him. I knew I was heading for home and it became my goal to reach New Zealand still as friends, to show him my country and then set him free. I didn't have the energy to fight it out with him. I still respected him as a person, but didn't foresee him ever being able to treat me any differently.

I achieved my goal and the scenario played out without too much hurt. We had toured many countries and arrived in time for a family summer Christmas in Mount Maunganui, in the north island of New Zealand.

We packed a tent and camping equipment and drove my little old Mini-Le car all around the South Island for a month. Shendon loved having a look at New Zealand and it gave me a chance to be reacquainted with my homeland, after having been away overseas for four years. Although there were moments where he tried to fight to get our relationship back on track, I did not yield and he gave up and returned to the UK.

10

Southern Cross ☆

Omicron has surged around the world and appears to have peaked in many countries allowing for mandates and restrictions to be almost fully released. Our delayed start to the spread of this virus here in New Zealand allows us to watch this play out and we see with some hope into our future. The larger daily case numbers will eventually peak here too and already our borders are opening to the world again, allowing for entrance without isolation stays at quarantine facilities, for returning Kiwis. Kia Ora friends.

Generally feeling peeved with myself that I had worked hard to make the relationship with Shendon work, then having it turn out nothing like I wanted it to, I decided to give myself a new goal in life. I was to get on without agonising over a love relationship, because I just didn't seem to be very good at keeping them.

Back in the Bay of Plenty on the North Island, in my birth town Mount Maunganui, I wandered up over the sand dunes and looked down to the surf beach with its creamy golden sand and the breakers continuously rolling in. I gazed out to sea seeing in my mind's eye all the other beaches I had explored through many countries around the world. What I now had come to appreciate was that I had actually grown up on one of the finest beaches out there.

As a kid it was my playground and I had taken it for granted, assuming most people had a swim spot like this in their lives. Mum would take the dog and the three of us kids on a walk over to the beach every day where we swam and dug holes and made castles and ate gritty sandwiches and leapt on our pet and fought each other for our parents' attention.

On the return walk home tired out after a few hours of salty air, Mum had invented a canny story to get our stumpy child legs back up the stone steps, climbing what felt to us, like a huge hill at the back of the beach. She had named them the fairy steps and while my brother made more gnome-like stomps up them, I danced up them, always attentive to any fairy dust I might discover. My baby sister smiled down from her vantage point in her pushchair or from high up in Mum's arms.

At the top of the stairs we passed the blue dairy. A dairy in New Zealand is the classic corner shop, selling the basics of milk and bread, the newspaper and most importantly to a child, lollies. We knew the place was full of sweets and icecreams and we longingly swept our eyes over it and then back to Mum to see if we could use some mind bending persuasion to make her go and buy us such treats. But alas, I grew up with a Mother on a huge anti-sugar march and so we were hardly ever allowed to buy any.

This same blue dairy installed the very first video arcade game machines in the neighbourhood and my brother and his friends would forgo the lollies to instead tip their pocket money into a slot to play a quick game of space invaders. This was also a banned activity in my family and I would be out on my bike all day spying on my brother to see if he and his friends would end up at this dairy so I could then immediately return home to tell on him, like a good big sister should. I felt it was my important duty to govern his behaviour at all times and because I had quite a naughty small brother, he kept me very busy.

Our best days were those when Dad got home from work so hot and bothered that he needed a swim. It was awfully hard for him not to take us (and the dog) once we knew where he was headed. So we would get a second outing to the beach and Dad, with his old surf lifesaving skills, encouraged us out deeper into the surf to swim with him.

Now wanting to settle here for a while as an adult, to appreciate what this area had to offer with its temperate climate and healthy outdoor vibe, I made a decision to stay local. I had experienced city life and enjoyed its excitement of constant entertainment, pulsating with humanity, but I now wanted to feed my soul with nature and a quieter existence.

Finding a little sleepout to rent, I got a job as an administrator with a shipping agent at the Port of Tauranga and allowed myself to spread out a wee bit more from the one bag of belongings I had in life.

A new teacher now entered the void I had created and I began a serious affair with the graceful movement system of Tai Chi. It dominated much of my leisure time and Mum, and the new friends I had made, were also all involved. We passionately practised every day, slowly ingraining the art form and learning about the Taoist way, including it within our lives.

Our club encouraged us to teach, and all of our teaching hours were done on a volunteer basis. We offered hours and hours of classes to the community each week, attended each other's classes, ran workshops, discussed Taoism and read and studied whatever we could find on the subject. We lived it and breathed it and stretched our bodies and experienced what it was to have a Master from the East come to visit our club and put us through our paces. We strived for perfection, not understanding at the time that there is no end to the practice of Tai Chi. The healing benefit of Tai Chi is that it fits your body on a day to day basis and the more you can give up on the pursuit of excellence and just get in the natural flow, the easier it becomes to move the intelligent energy (qi) around your system.

The meditative aspect of this form of exercise is experienced in your practice over time. First by the focus needed to learn a new movement where your mind has no room to think of anything else. Then as you learn the forms by heart, it gives your body an activity to do, allowing you to step out of your own way, giving space for your mind to find stillness. The execution of a set of movements known as a form, becomes a calming, peaceful act as you tune in to yourself at that given time and place.

With the frequent, repetitive practice of the Tai Chi you become able to perform the movement effortlessly as it flows out of you from muscle memory. To be able to remember which move flows next you must remain present and focussed in the moment. Becoming fully present you are able to feel the qi or life force energy in your body, and the slow movement gives time to perceive where your balance is and how the different structures in your body work. Students are often surprised with the amount of heat produced throughout this workout, coming from what looks like gentle exercise to an outsider. To walk away from an exercise with more vitality, balance and restfulness is a secret more people in the world should become equipped with for their wellbeing.

Tai Chi is also a language that teaches the harnessing of nature and what a beautiful place I now lived in, able to walk the beach, mulling over ideas and bringing nature back indoors by collecting seashells and driftwood to dot around the house on window sills, bookshelves or in small trinket bowls. I also tramped and camped with friends in the lush local native bush, rode my bike, swam in the sea and found my balance within again.

I thought the travel bug had tucked up its legs and gone to sleep under a rock somewhere or maybe even left for further travels on its own, leaving me to do the settled down part of my life.

Then annoyingly, a silly office flirtation for a bit of a laugh to test out those waters hooked an idiot of a man who, when I tried to end the affair, turned stalker on me. My lovely Tai Chi friends started being a constant presence around me for safety as we didn't trust him. It rattled me that someone once again had become obsessed with me and not quite knowing how to cope with the situation I once again decided to run.

This time the job advert was another tiny paragraph in the classified ads of a local paper and I needed a partner in crime to join me as they were after two people to look after a guesthouse in the Rocky Mountains, Canada. I had just the friend in mind and when I rang her she didn't need much convincing to give it a go. We applied, and were soon packed, on a flight to Vancouver and sorting our bus up into the Rockies. We headed to the small town of Field, 15 miles west of Lake Louise in Yoho National Park, population 300. My new fabulous address was Kicking Horse Avenue. The township lay in a valley between four distinct snow capped mountain peaks, Mt Burgess, Mt Field, Mt Steven and Mt Dennis, parallel to the Trans-Canada Highway and beside the Kicking Horse River, with a thick forest of trees carpeting the lower mountains and coming to encircle the town.

11

Keewatin (Cree, meaning Northern Star) ☆

And so in our larger cities we seem to have reached peak numbers of Omicron cases and the figures now trend down. Today after four months of vaccine passport mandates being part of our lives, we are now untethered from them. No more QR code scanning is required to enter a premises and so theoretically freedom of movement is starting to happen. Alas, many people are doing self-chosen lockdowns and restricting their outings to avoid catching the sickness.

The bus drew up higher and higher over mountain passes, where snow gently fell onto the road in places as we continued up into the Canadian Rockies. The stop on the side of the Trans Canadian Highway to let us off encouraged one other passenger to remark, "Gosh, is someone getting out *here?*". We jumped off the bus, shouldered our luggage and crossed the bridge over the Kicking Horse River into the dinky township situated in a large landscape. Patchy snow still lay in heaped piles at the shady corners of the steep roofed chalet style houses and the early spring air was sharp to breathe. We admired the odd, large, sleek elk grazing in a front garden. They ignored us walking by with our bags.

We found our new address and met up with Randal, the local park ranger. It was his holiday accommodation rentals that we would be managing. He was also invested in the Burgess Shale Foundation, and one of our job roles would be taking early bookings for the guided walks, led by geologists, into the famous fossil beds which were home to 530 million year old trilobite skeletons fossilised into shale, high up on local mountain paths. Randal lived alone in the top storey of his house with two self-contained apartments for rent on the ground floor. We lived down in the basement flat, complete with a large laundry area where the furnace was also housed for hot water and heating.

Settling into our new home with a well stocked pantry and fridge, we at first drew straws over who had the bedroom and who got the couch with a pull out bed. Staying close to home for the first few weeks as we staffed the phone and took bookings of the newly guided hikes into the fossil shale beds, we took turns to go exploring around the little friendly neighbourhood, buying a coffee and spectacular chocolate brownie at the nearby general store. A mountain spring season is a chilly offering and we were glad our accommodation allowed us to be snuggled near the furnace that was never allowed to go out.

Our guest house rooms were mostly pre-booked by holiday makers and we could start to plan the days where we would need to do the complete change over and have to be around to welcome the arrivals. We quickly found our routine of cleaning or freshening the apartments daily. Once we had the guesthouse clean and occupied, and the Burgess Shale Foundation had got its office staff employed, the rest of the time was free to us.

Borrowing books and maps of the Yoho National Park from Randal, we challenged ourselves to walk every available trail over the summer. Fabulous mountain and forest walks complete with exciting wildlife and high sweeping mountain meadows carpeted with long grass and new alpine wildflowers to admire and photograph took up much of the free days. We would pack lunch and walk for hours and hours, and our hiking fitness improved daily. Lakes full of glacial blue snowmelt added to serene landscapes, and fast flowing rivers washed over boulders into which we dipped our arms for a cooling off on a hot hike. Jogging home down the trails at a day's end showed us our improved fitness, remembering to make a lot of noise at all times to notify bears of our arrival, so as to not startle them, which is when they tend to act aggressively.

Our local territory was mostly populated by black bears who appear to be slightly shyer than grizzly bears and more inclined to run away if they have enough notice of your whereabouts.

Keewatin

One afternoon we chose to walk further afield in the
Banff National Park and we had headed up a steep slog of a
route to Rockbound Lake in behind Castle Mountain, near
Lake Louise. Arriving at the alpine lake surrounded by a
wall of rock that threw its reflection into the glassy silvery
green water with Castle Mountain towering over the scene,
we flopped down in the summer heat and unpacked our usual
picnic of English Muffins with cheese and mustard and some
fruit. Our fitness was at its prime and we knew we could
easily run quickly down the return route, so we had some
time to stretch out and relax and soak up the atmosphere for
a couple of hours. Finally, deciding we'd better head back to
the roadhead to hitch a ride home, we started our jog back
down the mountain route.

Almost feeling the noise blasting through my body
rather than hearing it, I thought it must be a landslide or
avalanche that was cascading down close by, shattering the
peaceful forest noises. I stopped in my tracks, with my friend
bumping up against me. We looked around and were startled
to be suddenly eye to eye with a helicopter pilot, the craft

lifting over the top of a ridge and flying quite close past us. We laughed at the fright it had given us and wondered at the sight of a helicopter as we hadn't heard too many around.

Continuing down the track we reached the road and didn't have to wait long before a local pulled over in his pickup truck to give us a ride back to Field. He then told us of the grizzly bear attack that had occurred in the Lake Louise area the night before. Six tourists had been injured after a grizzly had leapt on their tents at a campground near Lake Louise in the middle of the night, then mauling and biting some of the people. It was suspected a mother and baby bear had been involved in ripping into tents.

The campers were taken to various local hospitals, no one was fatally hurt and the loud yelling and screaming had seen the bears off. Park wardens had evacuated the campground and spent the day trying to locate the animals, using a helicopter as part of the search team. Unfortunately the bears were to be hunted and shot dead so as not to put more humans at risk.

Keewatin

Walking trails had been closed, but we had seen no sign of this where we had gone. Ignorance is bliss as they say, and we wondered if we had unsuspectingly been past said grizzly bears. We were both dying to see one, but not literally wanting to die seeing one!

Digging out old mountain bikes from Randal's garage to get us further afield, we became addicted to speed as we hurtled down some great forest tracks, ringing our bells and shouting our heads off to scare bears. We ended up riding out in some crazy storm days with hail and lightning cracking around the forest. A love of bike riding as a mode of transport has stayed with me from these days.

Because of visa requirements, our payment for managing the accommodation was board and food, so we both took a little extra side job for some cash up at another nearby accommodation which included a restaurant further up the highway. We worked different shifts so one of us could be available at our place if need be, to welcome guests and answer booking queries. We made sure we had some days free to go further afield to neighbouring parks and did lots of hiking around the awesome Lake Louise area within Banff National Park.

My Nana had been to Lake Louise when I was a child, and the postcard she had sent me showing the elegant historic hotel rising above the glittering turquoise lake had looked magical. To arrive at that scene for the first time was just like stepping into her postcard. It is a breathtaking piece of our planet and to add to its glory, it was snowing lightly on my first visit. For this visit, the lake was still completely iced over from the winter, but we went back to visit often and would sneak into the foyer of the beautiful hotel to quickly use the loos and gasp at the views of the startling aquamarine coloured lake and then happily head off on one of the trails. The area is heavily populated with tourists but the place has so much power in its beauty that humanity seems to shrink and hardly make an impact.

Miles up mountains with grandiose views over more mountains, in meadows dotted with yellow glacier lilies and clear running rivers, we would occasionally round a bend to find a teahouse serving cake and hot chocolates. The first one we came upon was like an apparition. What a wonderful concept. Your taste buds are on fire after a hard tramp, making anything you eat and drink that you haven't had to carry on your back taste ridiculously good. You are also happy to pay anything for the experience!

Tramping in New Zealand is an experience of connecting to the elements, but the wildlife is subtle. Native birdlife is mostly high up in treetops or soaring over mountains screeching their mountain parrot talk with the odd little robin hopping along a track to admire your shoe laces. The largest beast is a wild feral pig and they aren't stumbled across very often as they fossick for their food at night. To now hike in a country with so much wildlife was glorious. Hummingbirds, bears, mountain goats, coyotes, elk, hoary marmots, martens, gofers and a porcupine in full spikey quilled arousal are now all on my "seen it" list and I feel blessed to have been in their company for a short while.

Our guesthouse had a large garden with a patio set up with picnic tables and we would spend any sunny moment we had to be at home, up out of our basement apartment and in the sun writing letters to friends and family. Snow snapping explosions sung out as avalanches of snowmelt from the early summer warming fell down the four surrounding mountains.

I had kept in touch occasionally with Claude in London and of course had to let him know of my new adventure and wrote a long letter to him describing my new location. He wrote straight back saying he was coming to America for a holiday and wondered if he shouldn't add a week and come up and visit us. I agreed wholeheartedly and then, on the spur of the moment, we wrote to another girlfriend in New Zealand telling her we were receiving visitors and she on a whim agreed to come out for the same week. We made a rental car booking, pretty sure we could attempt the driving on the other side of the road to what we were used to in New Zealand and made plans for where we would take our visitors.

Picking up our rental car in Calgary we met our two friends at the airport off their various flights. Claude was sitting with his luggage on a bench when I arrived at the arrivals lounge. He had not seen me coming and I touched him on the arm and slipped into the seat beside him. He smiled and leaned over to kiss me on the cheek and it felt like we had only seen each other the other day. I introduced him to my friends and the poor man was now surrounded by three Kiwi women in an excited state at being together again. We travelled back to Field with lots of laughter and swapping of stories and gaping at views. It felt surreal to all be together in our temporary hometown.

I had warned Claude there would be lots of hiking involved for his time in the National Park and his trim figure held him in good stead to keep up with us. We did have a giggle at him when the brolly came with him most places - you can take the boy out of London, but he won't leave his umbrella behind. He had the tidiest, smartest outdoor gear we had seen in our lives and escorted him dressed in our worn out shorts, faded T-shirts and scuffed boots.

I loved seeing him again. He always had a soothing effect on me and it felt easy to be around him now. Our friendship naturally slipped into a more intimate affair and we were absorbed with each other's company whilst being surrounded by exhilarating scenery and good friends. It was a happy time for both of us. My interest in Taoism and Tai Chi matched his learnings of the I-Ching and his spiritual readings. We had much to talk over and it felt lovely to be closer to him than ever before.

The four of us hiked trails, joined glacier tours, sat by stunning lakes, ate out and fitted it all around our daily tasks of clearing guest suites and taking the odd booking. Claude happily cleaned the rooms with me and impressed me with his housekeeping ability. It was hard to separate us and we became more enamoured with each other.

Yet, we lived on different sides of the world and in reality this had to possibly just be a holiday romance. We made the most of every day and with a limit on our time together, it made every moment of the day seem very rosy and perfect. There was no time to discover the imperfections to our personas and it was easy to shine our best selves. We were outside our home countries and without normal daily

Keewatin

routines, there was a nice freedom to explore and possibly make up who we wanted to be.

And all too soon we were driving our friends back to the airport to catch their respective flights. Once again in the passionate sadness of parting, Claude said those words again, "If you're not married by age 30, give me a call." Marriage was not something I had ever chased after and the words didn't come across as a serious call to me, more like our little "in" joke he had remembered from my time living in London. We had taken our friendship onto a different level and yet I didn't ever see myself with a husband. The fact that he had never gone there either by this stage in his life must mean it was all a bit of flirty fun. I was nearly 28 years old and couldn't imagine changing my mind on all of this in two years time.

Both feeling pained by the parting, we rang each other with expensive toll calls to the other side of the world and wrote long letters regularly. But as two months went on it became obvious it was a painful way to leave things hanging between us. I don't think we had anticipated

146

becoming so close and therefore had to do some thinking about whether we followed our feelings any further. Claude could make no commitment to me, being so far away. It was too big a leap to be together in the world and yet I bounced between being cross at him and the situation and then vaguely hopeful we could pull something off. He was nothing but kind and gentle but I decided we should enact a parting of ways so as to not waste time pining after something that obviously wasn't quite timed right. We agreed to get used to being singles again.

The six months in Canada included for me some intense Tai Chi workshops with the Master of Taoist Tai Chi at that time, Master Moy Lin Shin who had visited us in New Zealand. In Edmonton I met with some people of my age who were just as passionate with Tai Chi and teaching it as myself. They visited me in later months near where I lived in the Rockies and it was fun to hang out with a young Canadian crowd for a few days. I flew across to Toronto at the end of my time in Canada and attended a week-long immersion workshop of Tai Chi and meditation which was a fabulous 28th birthday gift to myself. I also stayed a few days sleeping on the floor of the small centre complete with temple and headquarters where Master Moy lived in Chinatown, Toronto. I saw nothing else of Toronto and only immersed myself in Tai Chi, watching the magical master at work.

By this time it was mid Autumn and the cooling weather was nipping at my heels. Our visas were about to run out and so homeward bound I was for the Bay of Plenty where my parents still resided.

12

Starring Role ☆

The believable, reassuring, clear and calm tone of our Director-General of Health, Dr Ashley Bloomfield, will soon no longer be on our screens. Two years have passed since he stepped up into our awareness as a huge figure leading the Government response to help New Zealand through a world pandemic. Today he notifies us of his stepping down in three months from this immense role. Whether his advice was right or wrong, he oozed calm and logic giving a sense that his team were trying their best to assist the country. Bless you sir for the work you have achieved and you will remain a favourite figure of inspiration for many Kiwis.

Having settled into a good job as an accounts clerk within a chartered accountants practice and returning to teaching Tai Chi classes in my leisure time, my friend who had visited us in Canada suddenly threw a curveball at me when she landed a job in the area and said she was moving back. She was my sensible friend, the one who encouraged me to write up lists of pros and cons before I made life choices. Up to now, I didn't take too much notice of the two columns - I just ran. She now proposed that, as I had a permanent position with a good company and was of an age where I should be getting more serious about life, we should buy a house together. She had owned her own home in Napier and we could use the proceeds from her current house sale as the deposit.

I had no idea what was next for me and put on my rose coloured spectacles, made up my pros and cons list and thought what fun it would be to say I owned a house. I don't think I had thought too much about such a venture before, never believing I could do it myself. It seemed an opportunity was thrown down in front of me like a magic carpet ready for me to hop on and I decided to step onto it for the ride. The bank helpfully gave me the mortgage I needed and the location of the house we found was two roads back from the fabulous Mt Maunganui beach.

Starring Role

On the first night we moved in we had no furniture and slept in our sleeping bags on the floor of the lounge. I was coming down with a cold and didn't feel so great, and as my friend went happily off to sleep my stomach churned. I could only imagine it was regret that I was feeling - that somehow I had made an awfully big mistake. A sleepless night ensued and I had to take a few days off sick; I felt dazed by what I had done. The magic carpet I had stepped onto seemed to have been quickly whisked away from under my feet and I was now stuck in one spot owing lots of money every week back to the bank. I had a gnawing feeling that I had locked myself into something serious, when previously I had always given myself such freedom to travel - or run away.

I found I couldn't express this to anyone, as family and friends had all been supportive of my choice. I couldn't tell my best friend that I now hated my decision. I had to give myself a severe talking to: I had to suck it up and get on with it, remembering my self imposed rule to not regret anything I chose to do in life. So I made myself busy with work and Tai Chi to try and cover up my emotions.

But I anguished over it all as the year crept by. I was gently proud of the fact I was keeping up my mortgage payments and living on a tight budget, and I did love the location of our house for the ease of getting out on long walks along the beach. It was nice living close to my parents and to be involved in their lives again. But the unease kept surfacing and throwing me off centre. I also realised I was nearing age 30! I wondered if the meltdown that was happening inside me was the midlife crisis that everyone talked about when reaching this age. It started to worry me and I claimed to everyone that no one was to do any celebrating on the big day, as I wanted to just RUN AWAY for the big birthday day.

Feeling disgruntled with my lot in life I rashly decided to call in the long standing joke that had been running between Claude and myself for nine years. I dialled his number in the UK and when he answered in his lovely accent I literally groaned down the phone, "I'm turning 30 in a couple of weeks and I'm not married." "Well, well, well nice to hear from you," was his answer."Now what's been happening in your life?" I moaned and groaned how stuck I felt and how uninspired I had become with life and how I didn't know where to head off to in my future. He listened and asked me to leave it with him.

The day before my birthday in October there was a knock on the door in the early evening and a young guy stood there with a box in his arms. "I don't know what you've done," he said "but here's a case of champagne that someone has asked me to hand deliver to you." The message with the 12 bottles of French Pol Roger was 'Happy Birthday, see you soon, with love from Claude'. The phone call on my birthday from him, let me know that his flight was arriving in time for him to spend Christmas with us. He had a few weeks free and we could travel around New Zealand together to let him have a look around.

Straight away I embraced this turn of events. It would be fabulous to have Claude visit and to tour around with him. I didn't dare imagine that he was coming to propose, but I did have the odd daydream wondering what I would do if he did. Although I knew it was an escape plan, it was possibly too good a one to turn down. We prepared for his arrival and planned to host the Christmas breakfast inviting our families and having Claude positioned in the starring role. Pol Roger with strawberries dropped into the glasses was top of the list on the menu for the champagne breakfast.

The Boeing dipped down out of the early morning cloud and came in for a smooth landing and rumbled its way to the terminal. At the entrance gate we grinned at each other, pleased to be back in each other's company. Claude had the pale look of someone straight off a wearying flight and out of a cold dark winter. He squinted into our harsh New Zealand sunlight and breathed in the summer breeze. He had a few days to calibrate himself into summer mode and a timeclock to completely change before we would be off on our roadtrip.

He took one look at my clapped out little car and decided to hire a rental vehicle for our tour of the country. After a fun Christmas day, we packed up and started off on

154

our roadie. Claude eagerly pointed out sights that at first seemed mundane and ordinary to me, making it fun to revisit my own country through another's eyes. The big blue skies opened up to us and as we drove towards the South Island I also became enamoured with the scenery as I had not taken too much time down South in the more mountainous landscapes. We took turns with the driving and the daily travelling was filled with talk, catching up about our lives and every now and then hinting at what could be our futures.

Claude insisted we only stayed in motels or hotels and ate out at lovely restaurants, all of this making it a luxurious treat of a holiday for me. I started to suspect I had come up with my new route to run from my current life circumstances. It had a pre-planned feel to it and without too much discussion I had agreed I would make the shift to London and move into Claude's flat. I just couldn't fathom how I would tell my friend that I needed to move countries and didn't want a mortgage anymore.

Luckily the universe was in alignment with me and on returning from our trip we discovered another job had

155

come into my friend's life. She needed to tell me that she didn't want to live in our house anymore and was to move towns again. We decided to rent out our house while we took up our new paths.

Now fitting my life possessions into a camphor wood chest that I had inherited from my Nana, I sent it on its way over the sea while I set off on the long plane journey to London. My body crammed into the small seated space for hours suddenly rebelled on our descent into Heathrow and I had to grab for the paper sickbag to void the contents of my stomach. Pale and nauseous is how I presented myself for my arrival full time into Claude's life.

13

Star Crossed Lovers ☆

Our borders are gradually opening up to more and more of the world and we expect to become fully open in the next couple of months. Mixed emotions arrive with this news, as we have come to enjoy travelling our roads and visiting NZ attractions on our holidays that are void of queues and busyness. Is it wrong to not want the tourists to return? Many businesses in horticulture and hospitality are crying out for them to come back and be the workers. I have found it refreshing to have this little gem of a country all to ourselves for a while.

As the water ran over me in a refreshing shower at his small flat, I still didn't quite believe this was going to be my home from now on, beside Claude. He immediately offered me English hospitality by taking me out to a riverside pub for lunch. I was jet lagged and dazed and forced myself to settle my nerves and embrace my new country of choice with all it surely had to offer. The sun was weak in its warmth and in the current of the river swirled litter. I sipped a cider and tucked myself into his side, hoping that after I got some proper sleep and woke up tomorrow this would all look prettier.

It took a few days, but I found my feet again and began to absorb what was around me. The flat was tiny, on the ground floor of the terrace block in a leafy street, but Claude had at least invested in his garden. A landscape designer had planned out every inch of his plot and the mature plants performed a beautiful show of green nature. This small sanctuary helped me to gather my thoughts, although I did have to ignore the windows from neighbours overlooking the garden and the frequent aircraft on their flightpath right over the top of me.

The camphor wood chest arrived and I skimmed a few items off the top and drew down the lid slotting the metal closure into place. The flat was well furnished and decorated and I didn't feel like adding my own paraphernalia to the blend. I decided to choose to enjoy living in the different setting which Claude had spent years curating.

We started attending social gatherings as a couple and I discovered that I was never fully comfortable with the clash of lifestyles between his friends and my own way of thinking. These professionals were at a stage of their lives where they had worked hard to own and have it all, making their fortunes in this large city. Although they were friendly, I was going to have to mould myself into a more London version of myself to become fully accepted. I was more comfortable in the kitchen with the hired catering "help" than being seated at a grand table with the over jolly hosts.

Claude's life was sewn up tight. And rightly so, as he had lived on his own for many of these years. To now take a seam ripper to these stitches seemed harsh and yet if he wanted me in his life, he had to accept some of my outlook on the world and allow me to weave in my own threads into his tapestry. We bumbled through the first month and although he tried to cater for my needs, I continuously just bumped up against him. He allowed me to darn small pieces into the relationship, but never took up an unpicker himself to allow a true seam to open up to let me in.

I took on a busy temping job on the accounts team of a large law firm in central London and buried myself in work. Our leisure time together became frayed as I wanted to go dancing and out walking and this just didn't suit him.

The gulf between us grew rapidly and I never lost the awkwardness I felt around his family and friends. I harshly judged their way of living and their values and assumed that they were doing the same of me. Star crossed lovers we had become. We had thought we could become a pairing, but the routes our lives had taken before coming together appeared to have been far too different. To be together as a couple we had to force some changes to our authenticity and neither of us wanted to budge over very much. Weeks turned into months and we never got better at living together so we started to pick at and annoy each other, lurching through a range of emotions in this strange situation.

A chequered relationship with a girl from his past came to the fore and the comparisons between us were becoming too highlighted for him to keep quiet about. Being romanced at the thought of gaining me from over a long distance and over a long timeline, had made him decide to forgo this other friendship with someone, who maybe he should really belong with.

He became regularly angry at small things around us and I would retaliate back with energetic bitterness. It became emotionally draining and tiring to both of us. The smallness of his flat kept us wrapped in close proximity and a nervous tension pervaded every daily task.

Then the welcome relief came when he said he was off to buy tickets for our trip to join a tour to Tibet. He knew he wanted to take me - he always had, but there was now a condition. He was also going to buy me a ticket home to New Zealand. I had my brother's wedding to attend and he wanted to make sure I could be there. Tibet was to be our swan song - our farewell to the partnership that was just not working out. This was the proposal that I needed to hear from him. I said, "I agree."

He arrived home flapping tickets and grinning. Handing over the New Zealand ticket he said, "It's actually a return ticket as it didn't cost much more and you can decide whether you stay in New Zealand or return and settle in the UK."

I spent the last weeks before our trip pulling out the threads I had interwoven into his life and was bemused that this was to be the best breakup of a relationship I was yet to attend to. Strange that he upheld his idea of taking me to Tibet and yet I felt pulled to go with him. He still annoyed the heck out of me, but I had escape plans for when we joined our tour through Tibet. His company would be diluted, leaving me free at times to go off with other tour members to seek out the highlights of the "Rooftop of the World". We had to share a room, but it didn't mean we had to spend every waking hour with each other.

The first flight stopped over for a few hours in the sandy city of Doha, Qatar where women covered head to toe in black abaya cloak and burka took my attention, reminding me of a doll I had owned as a small child. The doll stood in

162

full Islamic dress atop a high shelf and very occasionally I would climb on a chair, get her down and gingerly lift the black cloak to reveal a beautiful yellow silk dress beneath. I would then carefully lift the face veil to reveal her eyes and then quickly put her back into full burka and return her to the shelf. She fascinated me and made me aware from a young age of cultural differences out there in the wide world. We were en route to Nepal which was where we were to join our tour group for a few nights before flying on to Lhasa to begin our journey through Tibet. Doha airport was small and we looked through the crowds to see if we could spot anyone else who might also be on their way to join up with our tour.

Outside Kathmandu airport the people welcomed us with loud shouts, wanting us to hire their colourful motorised rickshaws and we were whisked away to our hotel through the city grime of bustling lanes and streets, avoiding the odd sacred cow. Having spent a wonderful time in Kathmandu once before, I immediately felt at ease in this country. There is a genuine friendliness radiating from the people and the aged architecture of their buildings and temples once again gave me back a sense of wonder. Dogs and small children roamed freely amongst smokey cooking smells from small cafes. Rickety shacks down long dusty dirt streets each offered crafts for sale - a whole range of brass items, wallhangings, puppets, paper mache sculptures, embroidered items, antique knives, ethnic clothing and silver jewellery. This city felt alive and joyful, buzzing with trade, loud laughter, colour and blessed with the aroma of incense.

We rested for a while in our room before heading to the hotel restaurant for some dinner. On the way to our table I spotted a single guy sitting reading a book awaiting his meal. I decided he must be part of our tour and that he would be a perfect friend for Claude to hang out with, freeing me to do my own thing. He glanced up and I smiled at him when passing his table, deciding to butter him up, ready for my scheming.

14

Star Signs ☆

Everybody, at some stage, will be exposed to the virus. This message which comes to us from every country didn't feel very real for quite some time. My friend's Dad died today. He was in his 90s and as he had COVID when he died, he has become one of the statistics. RIP to him. It is interesting your passing will be added to the historic numbers of deaths in our country through this strange time. On the same day, our son informs us he has caught the virus and so far has mild symptoms. Another friend's partner has it and she is in isolation for seven days. Our Prime Minister has Omicron. All of a sudden it feels like it is closing in around us and we too will undoubtedly be exposed.

At the end of a day's sightseeing, exploring the alleys of Kathmandu, we gathered together as a group back at the hotel bar, seated at a large round table having an evening drink. Seated on one side of me was Claude who had spent most of the day with me and on the other side was the single man, who as I had correctly guessed, was a fellow member of our tour group. His name was Mark. He dressed casually, had a high forehead and peered through unfashionably large glasses, giving him an intensely intelligent look. Having a drink together was the perfect opportunity to be friendly, get to know him and then continue with my plan to fob him off onto Claude.

We all chatted about the day's experiences and amongst the fun, I decided to try and guess everyone's zodiac star sign around the table. Mark was instantly scathing of such a project and the instant I had got around the table he decided to up the IQ of the game by giving us some statistics to play with. Turns out he was a Maths teacher from the south coast of England. He stated, "In a group of 23 there is a better than 50/50 chance of two people having their birthday on the same day." Around the table we went again, finding out the actual birth dates of everybody, only to discover that Mark and my own birthday fall on the very same day. Everyone was amused how correct his stats had been and I was entertained that in upping the anti on my game, it had been his and my very own birthdays that fulfilled his prophecy.

His English sarcasm shone through the group chat and I grew a little worried that it was becoming obvious that Claude and Mark were plainly poles apart in nearly everything that was discussed. They both enjoyed the debating; alas I could see this was not going to be an easy friendship for them to fall into. But I had my Libran charm to pull out and was determined I could get them happy to socialise and spend time together, leaving me free to enjoy the tour.

Flying the route from Kathmandu to Lhasa the next morning I looked out the plane window and it was as if we seemed to skim just over the tops of vast mountain scenery. The aircraft was at the correct altitude but the landmass below us was as high as you can get on our planet. Rooftop of the world, here we come.

I love the first breath taken on entering a new country as you emerge through the aeroplane door. Exiting the aircraft in Lhasa it was more like take a breath and then quickly breathe again - where was the air? We looked around as we adjusted our movements to be at a slightly slower pace to enable our bodies to get enough oxygen.

It firstly struck me as a landscape of nothingness. The small airport terminal building was plonked in a barren scarceness of scenery. On the trip into the city, I was surprised that there was not too much to look at apart from big blue skies and far off hills and lots of flat rural land sparsely sprouting dried grass. The epicness of the landscape is so huge that the panorama outlook makes it hard to see. You are already at such a high altitude that the seemingly smaller hills are almighty mountains in their own right. The land was empty of people and dwellings and seemed so barren, having just left a hectic cityscape of London. This was desert scenery again, yet this time high up on a mountain plateau.

Star Signs

We all met up at our good starred hotel room run by the Chinese, as was the requirement for touring through Tibet at the time, and we were delegated rooms as per our ages. Not being ageist, our tour guide was simply looking out for the more senior members of the tour by giving them a ground floor room, as taking a flight of stairs at this altitude was like running a 400m race on the body.

We also met our lovely local Tibetan guide, whom I was pleased to find out was a woman and we warmed to her instantly. She presented us with a white Khata, placing it around our necks to welcome us and once we had settled into our rooms she led us out on a local walk through the nearby neighbourhood. Puffing slightly with the altitude we wandered through an alleyway of old simple mud brick dwellings. As though wearing kohl eyeliner, the windows being the eyes of the home, were outlined with wide black painted window frames. Sleeping dogs awoke to shake out their shaggy coats and trot after our group and small children grinned and giggled and ran away. Women dressed in traditional striped aprons over their long black skirts, representing that they were married, leaned on door posts and nodded to us and shyly looked down as we made our way past their homes.

The Potala palace would tower into view from different angles and a shiver of excitement ran through me knowing we would be entering the famous site in the next few days. The architecture of the palace is rustic and is softened by rounded corners. The many black outlined windows offer the imagination many ideas as to what fills all of those numerous spiritual rooms. I had no trouble perceiving that its magnificent presence beamed out incredible energy to the land and people around. The depth of feeling the local people have for their pilgrimage to the site and the manner in which many travel great distances, trekking and prostrating themselves along the ground, reaches deep inside you to quickly claim your respect. This was a site that had something to offer the soul!

I chatted to an American couple on our tour and looked over my shoulder to see where Mark was, hoping he was walking with Claude, but saw he was ambling along by himself at the back of the group pausing to take photographs with what looked to be a very good camera. Claude had the latest little shoot and go camera with a panorama option, so I was sure they could enthuse about photography together. I liked Jessica and James, the American couple whom I had just met, although they were quite reserved and might not have appreciated me always tagging along with them. I would spread myself out spending time with each of the other tour members if they would allow it. More holiday time and less Claude time was my goal.

Our tour was timed to be able to attend the Shoton (yoghurt) festival and on day two we ambled up a wide rocky path near the Deprang Monastery joining the throng of people winding their way up to a viewing spot on the side of a mountain. A giant Thangka was to be unfurled by a group of monks down the side of a hill. The crowds of Tibetan people would be throwing a white Khata ceremonial scarf out onto the brilliant coloured tapestry depicting Buddha, requesting a blessing. Llamas in bright yellow high crested hats sat across the top of the Thangka playing out the deep haunting, wailing and booming notes from the sutra bugles or long Tibetan horns, whilst large groups of monks sat chanting. Billowing scented smoke wafted through the people from large incense fire pits holding whole bushes of juniper.

The holiday feel of the day with families making the pilgrimage to the site and around the monastery felt welcoming and sacred. Small babies strapped onto their mothers' backs peeped at us, their little bare bottoms hanging out with no need for nappies. Large flasks of yak butter tea were carried to picnic on through the day and stalls sold yoghurt and snacks on the way.

I drank in the colours of the embroidered tapestry and monks clothing and ethnic dress of the people against the backdrop of cerulean blue sky and wafting clouds of scented smoke. I felt such peace in this setting and I had absolutely no fear of the crowds of people, which I usually feel in heavily populated settings. This country absorbed all of my attention and although it was a new experience I felt entirely comfortable to be part of the day's ceremony.

Star Signs

We wound down the mountain and entered the great hall of the monastery where more monks sat chanting in their extremely low primal toning. The sound they emitted stilled me instantly and brought tears to my eyes. I became aware of someone standing next to me, also transfixed with the sound, and found Mark was beside me. We shared a look, summing up the awe we were feeling for the environment we found ourselves in. The floor was greasy black with the drippings of yak butter from years of candles in their small brass holders and the whole atmosphere held a fetid, cloying smell that caught in the back of the throat. It was earthy, transporting, beautiful and very touching.

Celebrations then continued down in the town's streets with wonderfully chaotic opera performances entertaining large crowds of happy people. Claude and I wandered back to the hotel in time for dinner and then once again our tour group retired to the bar to talk through the wonderful day's events. Chinese brandy bottles scattered the tables and our tour guides happily entertained us with stories from being on the road.

Star Signs

One by one the tour group toddled off to their respective rooms for some hoped for high altitude sleep and Claude decided he would retire as well. I was too keyed up from such a great day and didn't want it to end. All of a sudden there was only myself and Mark left sitting at the low tables. Grabbing a small bottle of the brandy he decided we should make our way to the hotel roof terrace to have a look at the night stars. I grabbed a packet of cigarettes someone had left behind and we took to the stairs to climb into the night, having to pause at each level for an extra breath or two.

Stepping out onto the terrace into the starlit black night we were wowed to find an amazing view out over the town and up to the Potala Palace lit by dozens of dim lights. There weren't many words needed. We sat and drank and lit a cigarette and let the warmth of the night settle around us. "I think I've been here in a former lifetime," I bravely told him. "It all feels so comfortable and maybe our whole tour group have all been monks together before in previous lifetimes," I continued on, woozy from drink and cigarettes and excitement and the high altitude. He laughed politely and let me know he didn't share my view. But we had a few laughs and then tottered back to our respective rooms.

Once again on a rooftop terrace, but this time at the Palace in the clouds, I found myself looking out over Lhasa and the distant river and valley to more mountains and feeling so incredibly lucky that I was here at this location. The pilgrimage through the treasures of the internal Potala Palace offering so much to see, had been overwhelming on the senses. We had been ushered on at all times, to keep moving continuously through each room to allow for the crowds of pilgrims to experience this sanctum, leaving us not much time for contemplation of the huge statues of Buddha and the golden and silver treasures, intricate murals, and the former bedroom of the Dalai Lama.

The pause on the rooftop was a relief and as I wandered off Claude took a snapshot of me and in that photo walking up behind me is Mark. The three of us finished off the immense tour of the best Palace in the whole world and made our way back to our hotel rooms for a rest up after all the stairs we had just walked.

Making our way down the hotel stairs to explore for the free afternoon, we again caught up with Mark, also on his way out. We decided to join the locals and to circumambulate the holy Jokhang Temple by making our way through the Barkhor Street market, walking in the traditional clockwise direction. The stalls stocked any accessory that a pilgrim would ever need on their journey to enter the temple. Many people held small prayer wheels, spinning them in their clockwise direction, murmuring the required mantras. We came across the large prayer wheels and ran our hands along the heavy metal wheels to set them in motion and send off our prayers and accumulate some good karma.

Once again on entering the Temple, the sound of seated monks chanting, the smell of yak butter and the energy of the place threw a blanket of peacefulness around me and wrapped me up. The architecture was old and solid with many dark corners, yet shafts of bright sunlight rained through high windows highlighting odd parts of the rooms. Pilgrims worshipped alongside us tourists with no malice or worry that we were sharing their sacred space. Simple joy and peace is the environment I found myself in and it left me wishing I had such a place to visit in my own town. This tour was predominantly about visiting monasteries so I was to be in my happy place for the rest of the trip.

A couple of days into the tour and I was feeling that Claude was still around a bit too much for my liking, when unfortunately for him, he succumbed to travel belly. He was suddenly confined to barracks to be able to get to the porcelain palace when it called to him violently. Here was my chance to get out and do more on my own and yet more often than not, Mark would also be there. I started to hint to him at the situation between myself and Claude and let him know that I wasn't too sad to be off exploring without Claude at my side. In fact, with his lovely sarcastic humour, Mark soon renamed Claude - "Clench". There were days we had to travel long distances between toilets and there was nothing else for it but to clench those buttocks.

Four wheel drive SUVs were part of our transport options. We would be rumbling along a deeply rutted dirt road and then a driver knowing a shortcut would veer off down a seemingly too steep slope and through endless tundra and suddenly link up with a road again. Sitting jammed in the back seat between Claude and Mark I would suddenly find myself grabbing Mark's arm in fright with the sudden erratic driving. I did catch myself doing this one day and musing it was strange. I put it down to knowing how sensitive Claude was feeling and if I had grabbed him, it may have ended messily.

We would often have to exit out of our stuck vehicles and watch men try to get the tires to grip onto the road again and get us underway. The rainy season had left much of the tracks muddied and rutted and in a pretty bad way. Small river crossings were done with musings of the drivers as they stood around on the side of the river stroking their chins. They would jump back into vehicles and off we would roar with the hopeful blessing of Buddha, to leap about in the river and power out of the other side. Hairy black and white yaks grazing at the road side would stare at our brief noisy intrusion to their day and return to their busy eating of the short stubby grass and herbs.

Many of the days as we travelled between towns, we would be crossing over high mountain passes. The signal to show you were at the high peak of the road was the lines and lines of prayer flags attached to tall poles fluttering in the breeze. Their washed out colours were imparting messages of wisdom, peace, compassion and strength on the element of wind to permeate the lands around. At one such pass I took the camera from Claude and went out to the middle of the flags and lay down on the craggy bare earth that in winter would have been covered in immense layers of snow. I wanted a photo looking up through the sacred flags to a Tibetan sky. I heard a noise beside me and looked over to see Mark lying on the dark soil also getting the very same shot and grinned at him. I reckoned it was going to be the best photo of the holiday, once we got home and got the film developed.

Star Signs

With ten days touring we were now onto some big days of travelling long miles along the aptly named Friendship Highway to take us down out of Tibet and into Nepal, back to Kathmandu. At day's end we exited the bus and stood looking across to our highest mountain in the world "Holy Mother" Mt Everest. After a dinner of momo dumplings in soup we sat outside and watched a fantastic sunset turn the world a magenta pink and light up the top of the snow capped Qomolangma. Mark changed his film to slide film as he thought this was worthy of a future slide show. Mother Earth presented a beautiful finale to our last night in a magical country.

Our next day was the big haul over mountain passes on dirt and gravel roads down to the border with Nepal. The recent rains had wreaked havoc with the roads in many parts and we had numerous modes of transport that day between immense rock falls over which we had to travel on foot. Anyone who could drive and whatever transport could be summoned would then take us along the next stage of the journey. It was the most challenging travel day of my life.

Star Signs

The tour guide took a look at the concern on my tired face for one stage of our high mountain road (track) venture and said I could have a turn up in the cab of the battered open back truck, with one of the more senior ladies in our group. I sat in the middle beside the driver who was a young teen and watched him fight the shift gear and fight to keep the truck on the road over rough terrain. Meanwhile, enormous drops from the roof of the world fell down and down into ravines and gullies miles below. Our wheels teetered so close to the edges as my stomach heaved and I sweated and felt in a constant fright state, putting every hair on my body on alert. Having got through that stage we staggered by foot over the next landslide and once again onto some waiting vehicles.

This time I opted for the back of the classic blue Tibetan open back truck as I reasoned if we went over the side I had more chance of jumping off first. Rain began to fall and the driver leapt into the back with us and proceeded to cover us with a large tarpaulin. I made my way to the side of the vehicle so I could hold up the tarpaulin and at least look out over the side - eek! Down the huge mountain drops.

Claude was huddled on someone's luggage in the middle of the truck and I looked to see who was beside me to find a bemused Mark gripping the side of the vehicle. "Not sure we're going to make this," was his optimistic comment. In some sort of karmic retribution for nicknaming Claude, now every muscle in my body clenched hard thinking I had some sort of control of keeping our vehicle on the road. We were above the back tire and it rolled out over thin air every now and then. Hours and hours of journeying like this and I was beyond speaking.

Another avalanche crossed on foot and the next truck was a huge lorry where we were herded with our luggage into the large enclosed space and the metal door clanged shut as we sat in near darkness for the fortunately not too long next part of the road, wondering how close we were to the edge.

Slowly we bumped and rattled and jerked our way down winding mountain routes. The land grew more fertile,

182

forests appeared and there was such delight in reaching a river crossing with a serviceable bridge and here we stopped to enter the customs building. We were back in Nepal. Awaiting us was a normal small bus and we collapsed into the seats and off we hurtled into the evening towards Kathmandu. As it grew dark, it was just so much better to not know the state of the road. But this road was at least in a semi tar sealed condition and we seemed to be moving along at a pace.

Hopping out of the bus at the Hotel in Kathmandu, my body had seized completely from the tortuous muscle control I had been gripping and clenching with all day. I could hardly walk and my arms and shoulders screamed. I made it to our room for a long hot soak in the bath, so thankful that the hotel room had one, and I lay there mighty proud of the fact that I had survived Friendship Highway. I hoped with the epic task of travelling such a named road, that at least one friend had been gained. During moments of terror throughout that day it seemed it was Mark who was close by me and not Claude, who I hardly remembered seeing.

On our last free afternoon in Kathmandu Claude was staying close to the hotel room and so once again Mark and I met up and went out together, trekking through the market stalls on the hunt for a Thangka he wanted to purchase to take home. We marvelled at the very fine intricate painting done on silk or cotton and discovered we had a similar taste in which ones we thought would look good on a wall as a piece of Buddhist art. Deciding I didn't even have a home anymore and didn't know where I was to end up, I decided not to purchase one and just enjoyed helping Mark pick out his. The colours he went for were absolutely the colours we had just experienced in Tibet. It folded into a tube for safe travel and he would have it framed on his return to the UK.

15

Stars Above Dark Peaks ☆

While a whole host of other stories of the world gone crazy now headlines the daily news, we have to dig deeper to find pandemic news. Our borders are fully open with no requirement for quarantine on arrival into the country. Long delays in obtaining renewed passports are now being felt as travellers get prepared to climb into the skies. Aircraft are being dragged out of storage and airline staff are being enticed back to the industry. It seems we will not sit still any longer, we are driven to move about seeking new experiences.

Flying back to the UK, once again our short stopover was in Doha. Qatar aspired to then aid my life path plans. A mix up of the seating on our flight to London found myself and Mark seated beside each other, with Claude seated a few rows in front of us. Mark immediately offered to swap seats with him, but I insisted he stay put. Things were more and more fraught between Claude and myself. The end of our relationship was well and truly in sight now and it was becoming increasingly hard to be polite to each other. I snapped up the chance for a break from him and Mark and I sat in our seats chosen by the Persian cosmos ruminating all the way back to England.

The high altitude dinner choice for me that evening on the Qatar Airways flight was Seasonal Salad, Vegetable Moussaka with Potato Dauphinoise, Carrots and Courgettes followed by Mango Mousse. The hours of flying ticked over and the realisation of leaving a new friend behind as we returned to our homes suddenly saddened me. "I have 10 days left before flying home to New Zealand," I relayed to Mark. "Things are getting a bit stretched between myself and Claude now, I'll have to find things to do to get me out of his hair for the remaining days before I go." He reached into his bag and pulled out a biro to scribble something on the back of the dinner menu card. It was his phone number and another side note saying if he wasn't home, to ring directory enquiries for the telephone number of The Gordon Arms - his local pub and the next best place to usually find him. "Call me in the next few days if it's all getting too much for you," he bravely said.

Another foolish squabble with Claude saw me stomping off down the road from his flat to walk off my bad humour. I had walked past a phonebox and realised I had the flight menu card with Mark's phone number slipped into my bag. I slotted some coins into the box and dialled his number and got him at home. His friendly voice seemed pleased to hear from me and he invited me to come and join him on a weekend adventure with his climbing club up to the Lake District in the coming weekend. I found myself agreeing and he advised me on which trains to catch to get to his hometown of Fareham.

Claude puffed out his cheeks when I told him where I was going and demanded to know if there was something going on between myself and Mark. I argued back of course not, that surely it was the last thing I needed right now. I just wanted to go and see some of the countryside. He didn't seem pleased with me leaving him for a few days and yet he also didn't seem very pleased with me staying either. There was no way to win, except to just get on and do what I felt like doing.

Ringing the doorbell of the mid-terraced house on arrival into Mark's street, I got no response. Glancing down the narrow street, I recognised the sign for the Gordon Arms pub and wondered if, true to his word, I would find him propping up the bar. There I found him, a pint in hand and a grocery bag in front of him on the bar. Probably drinking for courage to get through my imminent visit, it was possibly the best place for us to break the ice. It's well and good meeting someone on the rooftop of the world, but quite another inviting them into your personal space. We toasted the upcoming weekend of getting out in the hills and he sheepishly admitted to having only just purchased the cleaning products to give his cottage a spruce up, but hadn't actually got them into his house to do their magic yet. I agreed to turn a blind eye to the bachelor state of affairs.

Stars Above Dark Peaks

The long drive to the Lake District with lots of tales of past escapades kept me entertained. We arrived at our destination at a stone club hut in Patterdale and met up with the rest of the climbing club members, all buoyed from escaping work on Friday night and heading for the hills. They eyeballed me curiously to start with but as kit got hauled out of packs and everyone spread out through the rooms sharing the sleeping spaces, I was included into the preparation for the next day's activities.

Getting out my sleeping bag and boots, Mark noticed I had exactly the same ones as himself. In fact on investigation we had both bought them from the very same little outdoor shop in Arundel. Beer at the local pub was next on the agenda and then back for some sleep, hindered by cacophonous snoring companions, awakening before dawn to be the first out the door for a day's hiking. The last of the stars were blinking out and a dim light began to creep into the morning. We wanted to get as high as we could for the dawning sun to alight upon us.

Stars Above Dark Peaks

Striding Edge was our energetic scramble to start the day and as misty low clouds wafted around us, I was thankful to them for softening the view down the sides of the steep slopes as we crossed over chunky boulders along a narrow ledge. Unlike its namesake, I was not striding along the edge. Reaching the top of Helvellyn with clearing skies, we dropped some layers of clothing, took in the vista and had a bite to eat. We were hardly puffing and realised that our time in the altitude of Tibet had given us a temporary boost of fitness. We decided rather than head back to the hut, we would stay high, tack on another few tops heading over the interesting named mountains Nethermost Pike, Dollywaggon Pike, Fairfield, Hart Crag, Hartsop Above How and down along a gentle slope back to the hut to make it into a round trip. We headed off, this time striding along with new enthusiasm and clocked up a huge day out walking.

Returning to the hut in the early evening where everyone gathered around sharing exploits of the day, I sat on the doorstep in the sun while Mark took over the cooking duties. I was offered an enamel cup of red wine and leaned on the doorpost in a body weary but blissful state that exists after a strenuous day in nature. Here was someone who enjoyed my happy place environment and in fact had way more experience than me in the outdoors. Here was someone who could challenge me to do more, try climbing, walk further and get into the wilderness even more often than I had before.

Bursting of that happy bubble happened on day two of the weekend and nearly broke me and almost quashed our blossoming relationship. A Grade 3 scramble, St Sunday Crag via Pinnacle Ridge, was the choice by my new mountain man. My glasses were steadily turning rose coloured by this stage and I naively followed him out the next morning and happily roped up and began the scramble, still admiring my new found fitness.

At a slight pause to catch my breath at one stage, I took the chance to look over at the mountains we had been out on the day before, then I looked down into the valley floor below. It was right then that my knees started knocking and shaking. My body decided I was way too high off the ground and the awful heebie-jeebies that come with the fear of heights started taking my breath away. I tried to cover up my anxiousness, but got slower and slower until Mark realised something was up.

Here was our first big test. We were three quarters up this thing and there was no sensible way to reverse and climb down and the top loomed still far above us. He had to prod and cajole and use every piece of his charm that he could muster to get me to the top. I veered through emotions of anger and wonder and fear and somehow bolstered enough oomph to get my shaky body to the top. The last heave up to step on St Sunday Crag was done in a non graceful manner with Mark hauling me up by my arms and I collapsed on the top and cried my eyes out.

I remember his startled face and I imagine he thought at that moment that he had blown any chance with me forever. For 30 seconds, I thought he had too. But a huge surge of adrenaline suddenly swirled through me and dissipated, then the sense of achievement bowled along after as I suddenly realised he was the most fabulous human in my life, for a very long time. Anyone who could have got me through the experience I had just had was pretty wonderful. To get to the top in one piece, I'd had to listen to him, try out his suggestions for foot holds and how to get a grip of myself and it had all worked out.

We were late getting back for the car ride home, but fellow adventurers forgive such behaviour and I was grateful not to have to do any of the driving, but just snuggle up in the backseat and enthuse occasionally on our awesome weekend away. Who were these energetic club members who put themselves through such ordeals in their weekends? They were RATs Club members of Fareham, Hampshire and I was proud to be a guest on one of their outings.

I overnighted in Fareham and once again Mark was the cook and host and we started discussing my open ended future with the flight I had back to New Zealand and the return ticket I had to come back to England. He said, "Use it - come back." I found myself agreeing. This time though, I wasn't running away from anything. I was running back for something - this was a turnaround and some new ground to cover.

I had a few days left before my flight and reluctantly caught the train back to Claude's flat in London. I wondered what the reception was going to be for my arrival back and it turned out it was frosty. It got frostier when I mentioned that my beloved camphor wood chest with my worldly belongings would no longer be required to be shipped back to New Zealand after me, but would just be doing a smaller journey to Fareham. He blustered and blundered on, questioning me about what on earth I was doing throwing myself at someone I hardly knew. I calmly tried to tell him all about my experience on the weekend with Mark. "Oh, do you mean Saint Mark?" was his cutting reply. Name calling was around again - but one I rather liked! I also quite liked his bluster and blunder, as I wondered a little myself if I wasn't being a bit rash and mad with my decision.

Driving me to the airport the energy calmed and we could both see the light at the end of the tunnel. Claude admitted to actually quite liking Saint Mark and thinking maybe I wasn't being too random with my decision and that even though things hadn't worked out between us, it had been worth having a try. We left each other in a friendly enough manner for me to climb aboard a plane and him to return to his bachelorhood.

My flight stopover was in Los Angeles for two nights and Claude had arranged, in what he had thought of as a kind gesture, for me to stay with close friends of his who lived there. In reality, it was an awkward stay as I didn't have the energy to describe my deteriorating relationship with their good friend. I played at a make believe life for three days pretending I was still together with Claude and decided to leave all the explaining for Claude to do after my departure. I made myself scarce by spending the days at the lovely local beach and walking the neighbourhood to get a feel for living in the American way. I quickly discovered that absolutely no one walked anywhere in this city and I must have stood out as an odd little figure making my way down streets with well cared for homes, manicured gardens but sparse on humanity.

Stars Above Dark Peaks

I had swapped addresses and telephone numbers with Jessica and James from the Tibetan tour as they resided in LA and they had asked me to contact them when I was on my way through. I decided to ring and they luckily asked me out for an evening and I could once again escape the tortuous game I was playing with Claude's friends.

James picked me up after work and drove me through Hollywood, stopping briefly to walk down the starred street of famous plaques along the walk of fame and then onto their small home to meet up with Jessica. I took some time looking through their albums of the trip to Tibet. I was really on the lookout for one person in particular, but he didn't feature in many photos.

I decided to tell them my big news and they were delighted over the fact that they knew and liked Mark and could enthuse over my new plans to go back to the UK to be with him. They talked with concern over what Claude was going through, but I assured them we were well and truly over each other and we were happier now we were over.

They treated me to a meal out at a vegetarian Chinese restaurant and I enjoyed being able to order off the whole menu for a change - fully vegetarian restaurants being extremely hard to find anywhere I had resided. I left them after a good evening out thinking that they were a nice couple, but doubting I would really ever stay in touch with them. I gave them Claude's email address as they thought they would like to catch up with him some time.

I now needed the cloak of Claude to slip completely off my shoulders - to be fully released from his influence. In a metaphorical manner of speaking it had been ceremoniously placed on me the day we met in the early 1990s and its metaphysical folds had swirled around me for nearly a decade. As I walked into the LA airport for my next flight home to New Zealand, I undid its clasp at my throat and let it drop onto the terminal floor - hoping it wasn't to trip up an unsuspecting person.

16

Reach for the stars ☆

Surging cases of two new Omicron variants make some news noise from around the world. We have them here too, but we are also well into winter flu and this is making more of an impact. Our traffic light system still requires us to mask up at indoor venues, but many activities are back to normal. It is now normal to arrive at a door of a shop or small business and find a scrawled hand written note informing of closure for a few days due to staff sickness. We shrug off the inconvenience and plan to try again next week.

Back in New Zealand visiting friends and family and enjoying my younger brother's wedding day, I found myself missing Mark. I had lots of time to daydream and was wondering how the next part of my life was to play out, including him in it and whether he was still feeling positive about our decision to be together. When speaking to my friends and family I had played down the part about him in my decision to go back to the UK and people close to me didn't show great enthusiasm for my choice to go back.

Our joint birthday date in October fell whilst I was home for the month and in the letter box a small package arrived from England. Mark had sent out a copy of 'Book One, The Eastern Fells: a Wainwright pictorial guide to the Lakeland Fells', as a reminder of our recent adventures together. The penned illustrations and local descriptions in this famous little book were lovely and as a book lover and walker it was the best of both worlds and to my mind was a perfect gift. Inside he had penned "Thanks for a wonderful summer and no regrets! All my love Mark xxx."

My choice to go back to the UK affirmed, I readied myself to return to the other side of the world. Taking a walk down the main street of Mount Maunganui in the Bay of Plenty had many reminders for me from time spent here throughout my childhood.

This was one of the towns we would come to from out in the country for our weekly supplies and to visit my

Grandpa. A beachside town with harbour on one side, pacific surfing beach on the other side of the spit of land and Mauao the lava dome hill at the end of the peninsular known lovingly as "The Mount" by the locals. The main street was filled with shops offering beach wear and surfboards and eclectic gift shops, joined by cafes and takeaway bars offering a cold milkshake on a hot day.

I looked up as someone was coming towards me and saw the face of someone looking extremely like our tour guide from Tibet. He did a double take as he got closer to me, obviously recognising me and we burst into laughter. "What are you doing here?" I asked him and he explained he was in New Zealand with a hockey tournament. "Why are *you* here?" he questioned, "and is Claude with you?" I explained my predicament and the ending of my relationship with him and then realising he was the one of the few people in the world who knew both myself and Mark, I also quickly explained our new situation.

He didn't seem surprised at all. "Well I saw all that coming," was his reply. "In fact, give me Mark's address as I have a photo that you will both enjoy. You are both on top of a mountain pass lying down on the ground under some prayer flags, taking a shot up through the flags to the sky." He continued, "That was a moment I wondered if there wasn't a connection happening between you both." He wished me all the best for a fabulous future together and left ambling down the street. I did have to turn around a few times to make sure I had actually seen him. This felt like another blessing to go forth with my plan.

Winging my way back yet again to England, this time I stopped over in Hong Kong, purely for the chance to land at the old airport Kai Yak on one of its last days of being in service. As a traveller, one of the topics up for discussion is often different airports around the world and this one always told of the landing flight path taking you almost down streets of apartment buildings with washing hung out on poles from their balconies and you were even close enough to spot television sets through the windows. It perfectly lived up to these descriptions.

A cool autumn day greeted me on arrival into London, but the biggest, warmest hug and smile was what I received once through into the terminal building. We held hands all the way back to my new home Fareham and on walking in through the front door and plonking down my luggage it just felt right. The very next day I was opening up the camphor wood chest and digging my belongings out to add my material worth to Mark's humble home.

A month after living together, the acceptance to his proposal was finally forthcoming in the orange glow of a very soggy tent on a grassy hillside in the Howgills, Yorkshire. A friend was taking part in a mountain race for the weekend and we had gone along for the ride and took the chance to do some walking. Awakening after a solid rainy night and unzipping the tent to more drizzle, we had talked ourselves out of an early start and lay dreamily cocooned in our damp orange nylon shelter.

"Okay let's do it," I said to Mark. He yelled, "Are you talking about what I hope you are talking about?" For two weeks he had offered me his hand in marriage with proposals at every opportunity: an opera, whilst washing the dishes, over breakfast, walking down to the supermarket and I could never summon the feeling to say yes. But this morning I had woken to a snug feeling that even on the uncomfortable hard earth we lay on and surrounded by the smell of wet boots and the odd drip from above, this was the guy whom I was happiest to experience all that and the rest of life with.

"There is a condition to my acceptance though," I had to hasten to tell him before he got too carried away. "We are going to have to run away." There was a small pause as he wondered how his poor parents were going to take on this idea and then he took to my idea wholeheartedly. "Where are we going to do it then?" he asked. "As long as no–one knows anything about it, you chose us somewhere cool," I replied. "I quite like Scotland," I added. He very quickly came up with the small settlement of Ullapool on the west coast of the Scottish Highlands. There was some good hiking in the area that we could clock up before getting hitched. We just had to check if there was a registry office for us to partake in our ceremony.

A wintery February half term and we were on a plane to Inverness in Scotland to pick up our rental car to travel out to the coast to our bed and breakfast at the end of a spit of land poking out into Loch Broom. Our bedroom window faced out to the icy wild dark waters of the Loch with the odd seal swimming past. Mist and drizzle swirled around giving captivating changing views across to snow covered mountains. The room was large and cosy and we unpacked our outfits for the secret event we had booked.

We had chosen our marriage ceremony time to be as early in the morning as we could, because we both thought we had quite a high chance of chickening out if we'd had to wait until later in the day. Before this nervously anticipated ritual ceremony we had a free day to get outdoors into the wintery conditions.

Stac Pollaidh was our destination for our last day as singles. The small mountain form reared up out of the land and came into view long before we reached the car park, its distinctive rocky ridge across a flat top with steep sides. The steep three hour climb started up a grass track and then took us up to towering sandstone pinnacles and an exciting scramble ended at the summit of the climb. We sat with the vista we had earned, warmed by the exercise but with any piece of skin exposed cooling very quickly in the icy wind, and laughed at what our world was about to hold for us after the next day's commitment.

We drove back into the village and found the registry office where we would be married on the morrow. We giggled to find our names published on the outside noticeboard of the building with the time of our ceremony. We had one mission left before this time and that was to find two witnesses who could attend the next morning to sign us off as married.

I had romantically anticipated finding two Russian sailors in the pub of this port town at the local bar, so we made our way there to see who we could meet. We had a couple of drinks and ate our dinner and no one appealed to us. The only solution we realised was to ask our B&B hosts.

We went back and found them watching TV and asked them if they had anything planned for 9.30am the next morning. "Only washing up after your breakfast," was the reply. When we announced we needed some last minute witnesses, they were astonished and then sceptical, thinking we were having them on. But with a little further persuasion, they decided the dishes could be delayed and they would happily escort us.

On February 15, 1999 we awoke to one of the coldest days I have known. The smells of fresh coffee and frying eggs greeted us at the prettily made up table. Grinning at us whilst putting down the breakfast plates, our host asked us if we were still up for the challenge. An overwhelming nervousness settled in my stomach but I nodded my assent, hoping I would find my voice when I needed it in two hours. We attempted the beautiful breakfast our hosts made us, clinked the crystal glasses and glugged down some champagne for courage and drove to our small venue.

The Registrar shook our hands and quietly welcomed us and I suspected we could feel her nerves. She admitted to not having done many marriage ceremonies and we assured her she could not have been as nervous as us! Our witnesses arrived and the four of us moved through to a small room. The Registrar needn't have worried, we had only chosen to go quickly through the standard readout and next minute we were signed and sealed as an official wedded couple.

We held hands leaving the building and to my delight snowflakes fell from the sky. This Kiwi girl had hardly experienced snow and so to have it on my wedding day was a blessing. Or so I thought, until an hour later it was hurling itself sideways with a vicious wind that blew my long hair out sideways from my head in our few wedding snaps that we took. We spent the day in a surreal state of newly wedded bliss running between a tea shop and the only restaurant we could find for our wedding lunch. Later in the evening, I sat in the window looking out at the storm raging around and made the phone call home. I laughingly said, "Guess what we've just done?" My Mum replied, "You've got married." No surprise really when for my whole childhood my parents had hinted that I don't bother with the big white wedding, but that I just ran away.

17

Cosmos ☆

And so to weave some final magical strands into my story…. Claude ended up marrying Jessica, the American girl from our Tibetan tour. When I had visited her and her first husband James in LA, I had given them Claude's email address and they had contacted him to show their concern for our breakup. They kept in touch with him and in December 1998 they headed to Paris for New Year's Eve and decided to also visit London and see Claude.

This was the start for their relationship, as Claude and Jessica discovered they had strongly similar spiritual interests. They grew closer through emailing each other, and visiting each other, and then, after a painful divorce, Jess moved to London in 2000. They married in 2001. Jessica's play time here on planet earth came to an end when she died in 2017 leaving behind Claude and their two children.

Cosmos

Over the years they had been together, Mark and I had moved to New Zealand and I had not been in contact with Claude very consistently, but I received an email from him to tell me of this sad news for his family.

It struck me then the cause and effect we have on each other's lives. At the time we are happily living our experiences, we don't really notice to what extent the ripples of effect are propagating outwards from each of the choices that we make. We come across 'fork in the road' moments where we could take either path to forge ahead and as we make those steps down the chosen route we take other people along with us.

Claude had been entangled in my life for a decade and although at first he seemed to be leading me up the garden path, he was in fact leading me to the rooftop of the world where eventually he became the bridge energy needed for the meeting between Mark and myself. I had only briefly known Jess for 11 days and yet I too had become the bridge needed to get Claude and her together. She comes to me now as a soft breeze. She was such a small part of my story and yet I imagine was a huge celestial star in Claude's story.

We take for granted that we have control over our choices and so too our destiny. But with hindsight, I notice that my life-path story may have been pre-signed and sealed, foretold in the stars by the medium I visited in the late 1980s who had been able to see it and read it to me. Was I in fact being guided and tested to always end up at this destination, having learnt so much on the way? What fun it is to now look back at a decade gone past and, without judgement on my younger self, just admire and gently chuckle at the choices that I did make at the time.

As you cycle through life learning its lessons, you come to realise that the occurrences which give you the blues and those most hectic of emotional times, are often the ones that spark off some wonderful experiences with people and places. What seem doomed as the bad bits are often the events kicking you into touch or over a goalpost to achieve something you never imagined.

The trick is to maybe not dither too long at any one thing, grab the moment, see the offerings being made and to show up each day and give it a go. My lesson to self is that it's okay to run away, as more often than not, you are actually running *towards* something more in alignment with the bigger you. Remain as light hearted as you can about the traumas, knowing that through darkness we are always tracking slowly towards the right destination - a place of more peace, where more light exists and where our true authentic self is allowed to shine. Change the fear of something into a sense of wonderment imagining what could happen next for the best.

Wouldn't it have been nice for my 20 something year old self to have had a visitation and lecture from my 50 something year old self. But then maybe it would have made it all seem too easy and this school of planet earth is not really about easy.

My teacher, seen in the stars a decade ago, had been a literal classroom teacher of mathematics. I had experienced many teachers in my travels, teaching me about emotions and different cultures and my self imposed limits and my challenges and my courage and my morals and my spirituality. Often nowadays, I find my guides and the universe to have a wonderful sense of humour, so I'm amused by the fact that the teacher on offer for me and seen in the stars ended up being a clever, witty, earthy and kind Maths teacher.

While I stick to the story that we have been together for previous lifetimes as monks in Tibet, Mark tells a different story of our meeting. He professes to have come back from his holiday in the Himalayas with 'excess baggage'. Either way, somehow I like to think our contracted agreement for this lifetime was to try a marriage friendship. And probably the reason for this was to present to the world another beautiful human, our son Bryn.

Claude and Jess did meet Bryn once. They visited us at our small cottage in Fareham in the early weeks after Bryn was born. I was acclimatising to becoming a mother, and at the time it felt slightly awkward and discomforting to have Claude sitting on the couch with my precious bundle. But now I like to think of it along the lines of a favourite childhood fairytale, Sleeping Beauty, where Princess Aurora's fairy godmothers appear at her cradle to bring gifts of beauty and song into her life. Claude once again alighted briefly in my life and maybe it was his presence that gifted luck to my son, as our boy seems to have had a charmed and lucky life so far.

Do You Remember?

The blue domes of Turkey
The whitewashed Greek isles
Ziggurat pyramids and tequila
All have drawn you far
Bright bold cities
Strangers and stranger worlds
Do you remember the walnut trees
The Christmas plays
The juicy berries and the wine
Have you found the dream you seek
When the monsoon is over
The mountain climbed
Will you go on to softer things
Violets, pansies, baking afghans
Or will the images call again
Different light, sound, tastes?

A poem written for me by my Mum in 1993, inspired by my letters home to her.

About the Author

Sarah-Jane has served in the Air Force, and worked in shipping, and in PR and HR. She has owned an exercise studio and a shop, been a librarian and worked with plants. Much of her time is spent teaching and practising Tai Chi.

She has lived in New Zealand, England, Scotland, Canada and the Cook Islands. Maybe she has finally settled down in Timaru, New Zealand. Maybe.